Discover The NEW

Best Places
To Kiss ™
In The Northwest

By Paula Begoun

Art Direction & Production: Constance Bollen
Cover Design: George Imray
Typography: Common Line Communications
Editor: Shellie Tucker
Printing: RR Donnelley & Sons

Copyright 1989 by Paula Begoun
Beginning Press, 5418 So. Brandon
Seattle, Washington 98118
First Edition: January 1989
    3 4 5 6 7 8 9 10

Best Places To Kiss™
is a registered trademark of Beginning Press
ISBN 0-9615514-5-3

This book may be ordered directly from the publisher:

Beginning Press
5418 So. Brandon
Seattle, Washington 98118
Please include $8.95 ($12.95 Canadian) plus $1.00 postage and handling for each book ordered.

PROFESSIONAL THANK YOUS

Thank you to Barbara Murel and Michael Hofferbert at Common Line for their skill, patience and more patience; George Imray for his wonderful cover design; Constance Bollen for her book-designing skill and advice and Shellie Tucker for her meticulous editing ability.

SPECIAL ACKNOWLEDGMENTS

To my creative sister, Avis Begoun, for the original idea; my longtime friends Debbie Gorenstein, Rick Pope and their children for the use of their home as a base camp in Oregon; and to all the starry-eyed people of the Northwest who let me interview them about their favorite kissing places covering over 5,000 miles of heaven.

DEDICATION

To my husband, Moshe, who keeps telling me that the best place to kiss in the Northwest is at home. I've tried to explain to him that a romantic travel guide doesn't mean you can't kiss right where you are. It just means that there are precious, secret places in the world, waiting for a loving couple to discover in them a new environment for cuddling and closeness. He still shakes his head, puts his arm around me and says, "It's a good idea, but our home is the *best* place as long as I'm there with you." Oh well, that's one less book I have to worry about selling.

PUBLISHER'S NOTE

This book is not an advertising vehicle. As was true in the original version of **Best Places To Kiss,** none of the businesses included here was told it either was being considered or had been chosen for inclusion; no listing was charged a fee or an exchange of services in order to be included. This book is a sincere effort to highlight those special parts of the world that are filled with romance and splendor. Sometimes those places are created by people, as in restaurants, inns, lounges, lodges, ranches and hotels. Sometimes those places are untouched by people and simply created by G-d for us to enjoy.

The recommendations in this collection were the final decision of the author and editors. Please write to Beginning Press if you have additional comments, suggestions or recommendations.

TABLE OF CONTENTS

KISSING
101 (Revised)

EDITORIALS

WHY IT'S BEST TO KISS
IN THE PACIFIC NORTHWEST AND
SOUTHWEST CANADA

I've wondered about that notion from the moment I started writing this series of romantic travel books. I began with the original Northwest kissing book two years ago and I have since completed two other kissing guides, one for the Los Angeles area and one for the San Francisco area. Yet, no matter where else I've gone, my personal romantic preference is always back here in the Northwest: It's not only best to kiss here, but there is no other place like it on earth.

There is a particular laid-back, casual, earthy style that accompanies kissing in the Northwest. You can feel it as you drive through the forests, along the rivers and oceans, over mountaintops or into the hearts of the cities. Perhaps it stems from the feeling of isolation from being so far removed from the rest of the world. Or it could be the informal, rugged outdoor attitude that goes hand in hand with the region, allowing you the freedom to let experience happen naturally instead of doing what is expected. That doesn't mean elegant and slick aren't abundantly available around these parts, but those types of circumstances, when included, almost always have a very specific Northwest flair.

Additionally, when you have each other and the splendor of miles upon miles of awe-inspiring sights to see, what else do you need? This part of the country invites you to be yourself, and because of that freedom, you can be closer to one another. A Northwest secret is, the more intimate you are with a given place, the more intimate you can be with each other.

You Call This Research?

Although it would have been nice, perhaps even preferable, I did not use kissing as a research method for selecting the locations listed in this book. If I had been smooching as I went I would still be researching. Rather, this book was undertaken as a journalistic effort and is the product of earnest interviews, thousands of miles of road travel, careful investigation and observation, backtracking to sites I had overlooked, and more interviews.

So, you may be wondering, if I did not kiss during my research, how could I tell if a particular place was good for such an activity? My sincere answer is that I used a more heartfelt part of my reporter's instinct, which allowed me to evaluate the magnetic pull of a place I visited. The criterion I used was: If I felt a longing inside for my husband to share what I had discovered, I considered that feeling as reliable a test as actually kissing. In the final analysis, I can guarantee that once you choose where to go from among the places listed, you will be assured of some amount of privacy, a beautiful setting, considerate service, heart-stirring ambience and first-rate accommodations. When you get there, what you do romantically is up to you and your partner.

WHAT ISN'T ROMANTIC

You may be skeptical about the idea of one location being more romantic than another. You may think, *"Well, it isn't the setting, it's who you're with that makes a place special."* And you'd be right. But, aside from the chemistry that exists between the two of you all on its own, there are some locations that can add to the moment, as opposed to some you're best off pretending don't exist.

For example, holding hands over a hamburger at McDonald's might be, for some, a blissful interlude. But the French-fry fight in full swing near your heads and the kid screaming behind you will put a damper on heart-throb stuff for even the most adoring of us. No, location isn't everything; it's when a certain type of place is combined with the right person that *unhindered* romance can happen.

With that in mind, the following is a list of things that were always considered not to be even remotely romantic: olive green or orange carpeting (especially if it was mildewy or dirty), anything overly plastic or overly veneered, electric fireplaces, an abundance of neon or ugly billboards cluttering an area, miles of clear-cut forest, odoriferous pulp mills either close by or at a distance, noise pollution, run-down facilities, factories smoking away at water's edge, tour buses, tourist traps and crowds.

Above and beyond these unromantic details there is a small variety of unromantic behaviors that can negate the affection potential of the most majestic surroundings. The following are mood killers every time: any amount of moaning over the weather, complaining about the quality of food or service no matter how justified, worrying about work, getting angry about traffic, incessant back-seat driving no matter how warranted, and groaning about heartburn or other related symptoms, no matter how painful.

RATING ROMANCE

The three major factors determining whether a place would be included were:

1. **Surrounding splendor**
2. **Privacy**
3. **Tug-at-your-heartstrings ambience**

This one-of-a-kind rating system was used as follows: If a place had all three of those qualities going for it, inclusion was automatic. But if one or two of the criteria were weak or nonexistent, the other feature(s) had to be really spectacular before the location would be included. For example, if a panoramic vista was overloaded with surrounding splendor but was inundated with recreational vehicles or kids on skateboards, the place would not be included. Or, if a fabulous bed & breakfast was set in a less-than-desirable location, say next to a cow field, it would be included only if its interior was so gloriously inviting and cozy that the outside would no longer matter or it would be impossible to remember that an outside even *existed.* Places such as these were always included.

Surrounding splendor is fairly self-explanatory. Heart-tugging ambience could probably use some clarification: Wonderful, loving environments are not just four-poster beds covered with down quilts and lace pillows, or tables decorated with white tablecloths and nicely folded linen napkins. Instead there must be more alluring, plush, or engaging indications that encourage you to feel relaxed and carefree instead of rigid and formal. Ambience was always judged by comfort and gracious appointments as opposed to image and frills.

PRIVACY RATINGS

If you've flipped through this book and noticed the miniature lips that follow each entry, you may be curious about their implications. First, let me tell you they **DO NOT** imply a quality rating. **All** the listings in this book are wonderful, special places to be and all get a five-star rating on quality and heart-pleasing details. The tiny lips are meant to indicate a privacy rating, a major prerequisite for romance. Kissing is not a spectator sport. Rather, it is a shared, intimate gift two people give each other to convey appreciation, love and tenderness. The amount of privacy you can expect to find at any one of these places corresponds to the number of lips awarded each location.

Good for discreet kissing only
   (restaurants and city parks)
Kissing and embracing acceptable
   (picnic areas or country parks)
Kissing, embracing and massive cuddling possible
   (secluded vistas, hikes or beaches)
Whatever the moment brings is up to you
   (your own private room in a B&B or hotel)

NOTE: Even though many scenic roads are included as good kissing places, it is not recommended that you kiss while driving. The kissability rating for these excursions applies only when you've stopped to look at where you've been or where you're going.

How to Find What You're Looking For

The Best Places To Kiss covers an area reaching as far north as Cape Scott on the Northwest tip of Vancouver Island and as far south as Ashland, Oregon. It includes the entire western coastline between those two points and as far east as the Cascade Mountain Range in the U.S. and the Coastal Mountain Range in Canada, and all the romantic places scattered in between.

To help you find what you're looking for, the book is divided into three regional chapters: British Columbia, Washington state and Oregon state. Each region is then divided into specific geographic areas. At the beginning of each section, the places are listed alphabetically. The descriptions follow driving routes or are arranged north to south or south to north as closely as possible. Finally, and hopefully, each place has been rendered vividly and evocatively.

There are also price ratings to help you determine whether your lips can afford to kiss in a particular restaurant, hotel, or bed & breakfast (all of the outdoor places are free). The price for overnight accommodations is always based on double occupancy; eating-establishment prices are based on a full dinner for two (excluding liquor) unless otherwise indicated. Canadian expenses are rated without an American exchange consideration.

		Eating	Sleeping
Very Inexpensive	—	Under $15	Under $40
Inexpensive	—	Under $20	Under $55
Very Moderate	—	Under $30	Under $60
Moderate	—	Under $45	Under $65
Expensive	—	Over $50	Over $75
Very Expensive	—	Over $70	Over $125
Unbelievably Expensive	—	Over $100	Over $200

WHAT IF YOU DON'T WANT TO KISS?

One resistance people I interviewed had to this notion of best kissing locales stemmed from the *expectation* problem. Some people were apprehensive that they'd travel to these places and once they arrived, never get the feeling they were supposed to have. They imagined spending all that time packing the car, driving for miles to the promised land, and getting there, only to not be swept-up, swept-away or feel even a twinge of romance. Their fear was, what happens if *nothing happens?*

These concerns are more than understandable because what is enticing for you may not be so for someone else. To prevent this anticlimactic scenario from becoming a reality, I've made some suggestions that might help: As you make decisions about where to go, pay close attention to details, talk over your preferences and discuss your feelings about them. For some people there is no passion associated with traffic jams, walking uphill in high-heels or finding rocky beaches when you wanted sandy, and there are some people who couldn't pucker up after spending $50 on a bottle of wine. How comfort or lack thereof can affect your lips and mood is something to agree on before you start your journeys, not after.

Plus, part of the whole experience is allowing whatever happens to be an opportunity to let intimacy reign. For example, remember the film *Body Heat,* and the incredibly intense scene where Kathleen Turner is standing in the hall and William Hurt is panting heavily on the porch and then he smashes through the door (even though it's unlocked) and rushes into her waiting arms, tumbling them both onto the floor? Well, how romantic would it have been if Kathleen had started complaining about having to clean up the broken glass, getting the door fixed or repairing her torn skirt?

So, if the car breaks down, the waiter is rude to you, or both of you tire out and want to call it a day, you can still be endearing and flirtatious. It only takes an attitude change and a positive loving viewpoint to turn the dilemma into delight.

WARM HEART, COLD FEET

More so than almost any other area in the United States, the Pacific Northwest and Southwestern Canada are at their romantic peak in the winter, fall and spring, when everyone else thinks it's time to hibernate and will venture out-of-doors only when the ski season opens or the summer weather is in full swing. Off-season not only provides reduced rates but it is the optimal time for truly unhurried, cherished intimacy because there are fewer tourists to contend with. Besides, aren't fireplaces, hot tubs and down comforters expressly preferred for the cooler seasons?

In the long haul though, this vast region is so spectacular it's hard to imagine that any time of year is not romantic. Each season has its own special joy: brisk hikes on a chilly winter day, mesmerizing fall sunsets, the rebirth of nature in the melting wet spring and the sultry summer heat to warm the air and waters . . . So during the off-seasons when the rest of the world is home in long johns and wool socks waiting for the spring thaw, you can be investigating the magic that hovers around every turn in this region. But note: That doesn't mean you should be one of those couples who avoids summer travel because it might be too crowded.

DON'T FORGET

Be sure to obtain detailed maps and keep them in the car. This prevents wasting time, wasting gas, and having frustrating arguments which can quickly dissipate the momentum of love. That doesn't mean getting lost can't be exciting, but being found definitely has its advantages.

One more reminder: This is the Northwest and as far as the weather goes, anything and everything is possible. In exchange for all this purple mountain majesty stuff, anticipate that the typical cold and misty-rain of this coastal-mountain region will prevail when you least expect them. Bring along warm as well as lightweight clothes, and, it goes without saying (though I'll say it anyway), always bring your rain gear, just in case.

What To Do About Crowds

Believe it or not, some people think congested city downtowns, airports, cab rides and sightseeing tours are romantic. Your initial reaction to that information may be to wonder what's wrong with these people and when was their release date? Have they never retrieved two weeks' worth of over-packed luggage from a baggage carousel with 200 other over-tired passengers? Waited an hour in line at a tourist attraction to eat a $5.00 sandwich wrapped in plastic? Taken a cross-town cab ride that cost almost as much as a dinner, not including tip?

On closer inspection these crowd-lovers are people who, by their very nature, are blurry-eyed, die-hard romantics. These rare specimens of humankind have a unique ability to blot out the world around them and see only each other. These purists with stars in their eyes know something very special, that love and romance are not limited to stereotypic scenes of roses and candlelight and are not impossible during a grocery trip or while stuck in traffic. They see that the beauty of the moment depends solely on the creativity they bring to it.

VANCOUVER ISLAND and THE GULF ISLANDS

VANCOUVER ISLAND

continues

The above listings are alphabetical for each island. The descriptions that follow are arranged north to south.

VANCOUVER ISLAND

Traveling to Vancouver Island is an unconditional *romantic must*, because, to put it simply, there is everything here two people in love could want to share. The island is a huge landmass resplendent with forest, a continental-styled city, miles upon miles of wilderness, rugged coast, fishing villages, sandy white beaches, rustic lodges, quaint bed & breakfasts, magnificent bed & breakfasts and a mountain range that spans nearly the entire length and width of this 300-mile-long stretch.

Narrowing down the entries for the island's best places for romantic interaction was a struggle because almost every acre is distinctively attractive and interesting. The northern central section is mostly uninhabited and thus full of untouched mountain terrain, wildlife and reverend scenery. The eastern coastal areas are marbled with long lazy beaches and dense-forested hills and meadows. The western coast is entirely true wilderness and thick forest except for the affable fishing villages of Tofino and Ucluelet. The city of Victoria, on the southern tip of the island, sets the ultimate contrast to the natural wonders, being endowed with old-world flourishes and memories and sightseeing paraphernalia on every corner. Along the southwestern coast, the unfettered, pristine quality of the island is again apparent in rocky beaches and provincial forestland.

This variety of terrain and culture may make it difficult for you to decide where to go first. But at least one thing is clear: You have to start by ferryboat. There are only four ferry landings on the island for boats arriving from the States and Canada. Check with either the British Columbia Ferries, (604) 669-1211, or the Washington State Ferries, (206) 464-6400, for scheduled departures and fares.

Cape Scott Park

From the Nanaimo ferry dock take Highway 19 north to Port Hardy. Just south of town, there is a poorly marked logging road that you follow for 28 miles, to the end of the road. You will pass a government-run meteorology station as you proceed to the parking area, which sits at the head of the trail. A very short climb reveals the path.

Cape Scott Park will feel like the end of the world because, for all intents and purposes, on Vancouver Island, it is. This park is the *epitome* of wilderness. Cape Scott is on the northwest tip of the island and is accessible only by a miserable, dusty gravel-and-stone logging road. The park is not all that far from Port Hardy, but because of the road's condition, the drive will take longer than you'd like. At the end though, you will be ecstatic you survived the ordeal.

When you locate the beginning of the hiking trail, you will be witness to a dreamlike transition from the gravel-pit road to an elfin land filled with the spirits of nature. A flat walkway of wood planks is the only sign of civilization, including people, you probably will see all day. Because of this, Cape Scott is the only outdoor place to receive a kissing (privacy) rating of four lips. You are guaranteed that much privacy.

From the trail head, you meander for two miles through trees wardrobed in moss and streamed in sunlight. Your path finally opens to an enormous sand-laden horseshoe around a bay called San Josef, which you can claim exclusively for yourselves. The waves landing on the beach fill the air with a rhythmic pounding. The U-shaped boundary is marked by forested hills where very few people have gone before. The innocence found here has much to offer the daring soul and city-weary senses.

NOTE: Because Cape Scott is a remote location, before heading out there, acquire a detailed map and complete information from the visitor center in Port Hardy.

WARNING: Before you begin to explore the bay, be sure to mark where you leave the trail or it will be tricky to find that spot again.

STRATHCONA PARK & LODGE 💋💋💋💋

P.O. Box 2160, Campbell River V9W 5C9
(604) 286-3122
Reasonable

Just north of Campbell River, take Highway 28 west for 30 miles to the Lodge.

When I arrived at the Lodge, having driven along a winding mountain road into the core of Vancouver Island to get there, I walked up to the reception desk and the first words out of my mouth were, *"What is this place?"* The answer to that question is, *"Like no other place on earth!"* The red, hewn buildings of the Lodge are set at the edge of a crystal-clear mountain lake embraced by an astounding procession of overlapping snowcapped peaks. Strathcona is without question a visual paradise. There are also no other facilities around for miles, and that has an enchantment all its own.

The staff of Strathcona Lodge are dedicated to introducing all who venture into their realm to the mysteries and excitement of the outdoors — to what participating in and loving the outdoors is all about. They offer guided instruction for any mountain or water activity you could wish for: kayaking, rappelling from cliffs, glissading down glaciers, wildlife hiking, canoeing, fishing, sailing and camping. Their brochure is a rare selection of packaged challenges for all ages and skill levels.

I know — that all sounds great but not necessarily romantic, unless of course you're Paul Bunyan on a date, or parents trying to keep your kids busy. But after I explored the lodge and the rustic cabins around the lake, observed the three hearty meals served family-style daily, and noticed that the Lodge does offer a honeymoon package, I was convinced that this was an extraordinary place for an outdoor-loving couple. There is actually nothing quite like it anywhere else in the Northwestern U.S. or Southwestern Canada. For that reason alone, your outdoor fantasies would be fulfilled at Strathcona Lodge.

THE OLD HOUSE RESTAURANT

1760 Riverside Lane, Courtenay V9N 8C7
(604) 338-5406
Moderate to Expensive

Heading north along Highway 19, as you approach the town of Courtenay, turn west at the first major intersection, which is the 17th Street Bridge. Immediately after turning, you turn right again onto Riverside Lane, the road just before the river. The Old House Restaurant will be the first house on your left.

As you drive up to the striking brick mansion that houses the Old House Restaurant, be sure you ignore the nearby train tracks and awful dirt road, because once inside you won't know an outside exists. This well-known Vancouver Island spot is a magnificent place to dine. You enter a room dominated by two stone fireplaces framed by wood mantels. Antique furnishings, and leaded-glass windows that line the back of the room, reflect warmth, gentility and rustic elegance. Plus, the food just happens to be some of the best on the island. Fresh, epicurean dishes with daring, unique sauces are the hallmarks of the kitchen. Certainly, if you find yourselves traveling through Courtenay on your way to the northern end of the island, this would be a memorable stop for both of you.

♦ *ROMANTIC SUGGESTION:* Twenty-five minutes from Courtenay is **Forbidden Plateau's summer chair lift, open June 5 through September 5; 2050 Cliff Avenue, Courtenay, V9N 2L3, (604) 334-4744.** As you dangle above the golden land below, you can study the scenic Comox Valley, the Strait of Georgia and the Beaufort Mountain Range.

Tigh-Na-Mara

R.R. #1, Parksville V0R 2S0
(604) 248-2072
Expensive

Just off Highway 19 on the east side of the road a few miles north of downtown Parksville.

If there were awards for impossible-to-understand names of restaurants and lodgings, this one would take the prize. Yet, if there were awards for excellence in accommodations, setting, views and dining facilities, Tigh-Na-Mara would walk away with, at the very least, an honorable mention.

And there is so much here to mention and praise — the clusters of log cabins interspersed among pinery and red-barked trails . . . roomy interiors with broad stone fireplaces that keep things glowingly warm. The restaurant, set in a log mansion, conjures up a consistently rich dining experience with attention to comfort, and serves delectable, fresh continental dishes, hearty breakfasts and lunches. And then there are the recently added suites that lord over the shoreline and the landscape of the mainland. These units were created only with lovers in mind. The sliding glass door to your private deck opens on a ringside view of the shore. Inside, the extensive living room has a fireplace, a hot tub and a silky new comforter for the queen-size bed. All in all, even though the name might put you off, the place itself has a seductive pull that can't be ignored.

◆ **ROMANTIC OPTION:** Up the road from Tigh-Na-Mara an uncommon dining experience awaits you at **Ma Maison, 393 Island Highway North, Parksville V0R 2S0, (604) 248-5859** (Moderate). This adorable, polished restaurant has an enviable view of the water and an enviable menu presentation of classic dishes prepared with fastidious attention to detail and freshness. A leisurely meal at sunset will be as romantic a meal as you could ask for along the coast.

◆ *SECOND ROMANTIC OPTION:* Next door to Ma Maison is **Heron's restaurant in the Bayside Inn Hotel, 240 Dogwood Street, Parksville V0R 2S0, (604) 248-8333** (Breakfast/Reasonable; Dinner/Expensive). I'm a believer that breakfasts are romantic; that is, if they are leisurely, classy and accompanied by a resplendent view and a significant other. Even though the Bayside Inn is in essence just a hotel with very nice hotel-like rooms and amenities, its restaurant is a three-tiered show-case, with all the right touches to make brunch here a must.

TOFINO

The 75-mile trip west on Highway 4 across the central mountains of Vancouver Island takes you to the remote side of the island. For the last few miles of this panoramic drive, the rocky coast chaperones your passage as you descend back down to sea level. When you finally reach road's end, the highway will split toward two towns: to the north is Tofino and to the south, Ucluelet. Which town you choose to sight-see in is a toss-up. Both towns are basically fishing villages and whale watching ports of call. They also pride themselves on being non-commercial places where you can charter boats for fishing and water tours. But for heart-stealing pursuits, Tofino is your destination.

Tofino is what a small town should be, unpretentious, with amiable unruffled streets and neighborhoods set like constellations along the volatile waterfront and the marinas of the calm inner bay. Every corner provides an escape, far from the madding crowd. Along the main road into Tofino, there are several waterfront resorts that line the shore and have unobstructed views of the beach and ocean. In town there are a few basic shops and casual restaurants. Nothing here gets in the way of the scenery or the ease of the area. Get close, kick back and discover that you're in a place where time floats by to a melody you can learn to hum together.

◆ **ROMANTIC OPTION:** Along the west coast, between Tofino and Ucluelet, **Long Beach** offers an abundance of everything restless surf-lovers could want. This location is defined by rocky cliffs, smooth, white-sanded beaches and forested picnic and hiking areas adjacent to the shoreline. The romantic possibilities are many; you can relax, walk along the extensive beach, hike through the forest that borders the shore and seek the water for a salty frolic.

NOTE: The tourist season here is so brief,. occurring mostly in July and August, that there are many months when it will be only the two of you, and the rest of the world will be somewhere else.

HOT SPRINGS COVE

Coastal Adventures, 1119 Pacific Rim Highway, Tofino V0R 2Z0
(604) 725-3777
Expensive

Coastal Adventures is a boat charter business that can take you out to the Cove. Call for reservations and directions to the marina where you meet the boat.

Coastal wilderness is normally available only to those who have the luxury of owning a sea-worthy vessel that they know how to navigate along remote, unpopulated shores of the ocean. But those people fortunate enough to find themselves in Tofino can take advantage of the daily round-trip excursions out to Hot Springs Cove, and what a trip it is. After leaving the marina, you travel for an hour and a half by boat amid the exquisite scenery of Clayoquot Sound as you head north for Shelter Inlet. Other than by boat, there is no easily accessible way to reach this destination, so, to say the least, this is one remote hot springs.

Once you dock, a half-hour hike through lush forest takes you to the steaming mists of the cove. The warm, cascading water spills over rocky formations into a series of natural pools. As you soak away the last bits of tension in your neck and shoulders, lean back and watch the ocean waves crash onto the nearby shore. This natural shower is bound to be one you won't ever forget.

NOTE: You have to bring your own water or drinks, there are no supplies available. There are campgrounds a short distance from the Cove should you desire to stay overnight and treat yourself to an early-morning rinse.

OCEAN PACIFIC WHALE CHARTERS

Box 590, Tofino V0R 2Z0
(604) 725-3919
Moderate

Call Ocean Pacific for reservations and directions to the marina where you meet your boat.

Take it from a skeptic — whale watching is romantic. Imagine yourself and your loved one staring out from the bridge of a boat at the Pacific Ocean lined with staggered cliffs haloed in forests of deep green. The coolness of the morning air swirls around you and you squeeze each other close for protection against the chill. You both slowly scan the calm, flowing blue motion and your thoughts are filled with the vastness before you. Then suddenly, in the distance, breaking the stillness of a sun-drenched winter day, a spout of water explodes from the ocean surface followed by a giant arching black profile, finalized by an abrupt tail slap that disappears into stillness once more. Believe me, if you're not standing next to someone you care about, you're likely to grab the person nearest you and yell, *"Wow, look at that!"*

Maybe it's the excitement of knowing that such an immense, powerful creature can glide so effortlessly through the water with playful agility and speed. Or could it be the chance of "connecting" with a civilized mammal that knows the secret depths of the aquatic world we mere mortals can only briefly visit and barely understand. Whatever the reason, the search is one you need to share with someone special. Together you can contemplate what to anyone's way of thinking is surely a miracle.

NOTE: During the whales' spring migration and summer feeding periods, thousands of them are to be found in Tofino's calm inland waters.

OCEAN VILLAGE BEACH RESORT 🙶🙶🙶🙶

Box 490, Hellesen Drive, Tofino V0R 2Z0
(604) 725-3755
Expensive

On Highway 4 two miles south of Tofino, look for the sign on the west side of the road pointing the way to the Resort.

There is nothing fancy about the two-dozen, handsome, cedar-wood cabins that make up the accommodations of Ocean Village, but the view, location and privacy are another story. Eight of these units are individual huts stationed in a row on McKenzie Beach. The entrance to each of these private residences is a sliding glass door that fronts onto the sand, wind and waves. Beachcombing, whale watching, hunting for seashells, building sand castles, playing in the surf, or listening to the waves lapping against the shore are some of the more strenuous activities you can find within inches of your door, and for miles in either direction. This place may not be fancy, but who needs fancy when you have a front yard like the one at Ocean Village?

♦ **ROMANTIC OPTION:** Down the beach from Ocean Village is **Crystal Cove Beach Resort, Box 559, Tofino V0R 2Z0, (604) 725-4213** (Moderate to Expensive), set on a quiet inlet next to McKenzie Beach. The log cabins here are lovely and well worth the stay if units 1, 2 and 3 are available. The resort is much like Ocean Village except these units are charming, complete with fireplaces and cozy interiors, which make for some of the best snuggling you may uncover or cover under in Tofino.

CHESTERMAN'S BEACH
BED & BREAKFAST

1345 Chesterman's Beach Road, Box 72, Tofino V0R 2Z0
(604) 725-3726
1 Couple/Moderate; 2 Couples/Inexpensive

Call for reservations and directions.

Oceanfront bed & breakfasts are a treat for two predictable reasons. First, the proximity to the ocean is enthralling and second, the luxury of a delectable morning meal is enhanced wonderfully when an endless shoreline happens to be the backdrop. Sitting out on the deck, you can feel the breeze lift the sea air all around you. The cool mist tingles against your cheek and as you sip hot, fresh coffee the steam briefly warms your face. After breakfast, a sentimental stroll, hand in hand through the surf, can continue on and on without interruption.

Chesterman's has three rustic units: a large cabin with a private yard, a balcony room adjacent to the house and a two-bedroom section of the home with a private entrance. All are viable options for a romantic sojourn in this part of the world.

WICKANINNISH RESTAURANT

Box 946, Ucluelet V0R 3A0
(604) 726-7706
Reasonable to Moderate

Fifteen miles south of Tofino, on Highway 4, look for signs on the west side of the road that will direct you to the restaurant and Interpretive Centre.

This is not your typical kind of kissing place. Wickaninnish is the name of an outstretched beach with hundreds of weathered logs strewn like toothpicks along the shore. There is also a large wood building by the same name that houses an information center, a museum of Indian culture and a restaurant located on the edge of the sandy shore. The information center and museum, together known as the Interpretive Centre, are educational points of interest, but hardly romantic, unless of course you want to kiss an artifact. The restaurant, on the other hand, is exceptionally romantic, particularly during off-season when the tourists are home waiting patiently for the summer.

The restaurant is encircled by windows that showcase the beach and the ever-changing status of the shore. Threatening winter storms, dramatic high tides and motionless summer days create a changeable landscape that is at one moment languid and silent and the next violent and thundering. Regardless of what excitement nature is providing, the Wickaninnish Restaurant will serve you gracious meals while you sit back and watch the show.

NOTE: Weather permitting, after lunch, this is truly a perfect place to hike along the beach or through the woods behind the back of the building. When you're done, a toast to the day you shared together will be waiting back at the restaurant.

CROW AND GATE

Yellow Point Road, Ladysmith V0R 2E0
(604) 722-3731
Inexpensive

About three miles north of Ladysmith on the Island Highway, turn right on Cedar Road and then turn right at the second entrance to Yellow Point Road. Travel for one mile to the restaurant which is on the right side of the road. Follow the signs from Island Highway if you get confused.

Among the pines, nestled in the rolling meadows of the countryside, dabbed with rose gardens and spiced with ale, you'll find the ambience of another era in an English-styled restaurant called the Crow and Gate. The setting of this cottage, on the pastoral east coast of Vancouver Island, provides a momentary refuge for weary, hungry travelers looking for an inn that is really an inn.

Here you'll find the pleasure of the past as you take your tea at a table near the stone hearth and let your visit shape itself. The food is traditional British fare, with the accent on fresh, hearty and friendly. So snuggle close together, watch the embers flicker and glow in the dimly lit room, as you wait for the innkeeper to fetch your afternoon or evening meal.

YELLOW POINT LODGE

R.R. 3, Ladysmith V0R 2E0
(604) 245-7422
Reasonable

Call for reservations and directions to the Lodge.

What can I say, I made new reservations before I left. This was as inviting a location as I could have wanted for time away to do nothing more than decide what to wear to the three wonderful meals and the three teas served daily in the handsome main lodge. Why the hurry to sign up again? First, it's hard to get a reservation. This popular B.C. getaway is well-known for several reasons: its remote location on one mile of beaches and secluded coves bordered by 180 acres of forest; the care of the staff; the delicious meals; and its ability to truly relax you. This is a desirable, beautiful place for the heart, mind and soul.

Your lodging choices here are best described as eclectic. The ones for romantic interaction are the new log cabins that line the shore, tucked among pines and hidden from view. There are more rustic accommodations scattered around the extensive property with assorted price ranges. But you'll find, once you arrive there, that the question at Yellow Point Lodge is not where to stay — it's when can you come back.

FAIRBURN FARM COUNTRY MANOR

R.R. #7, Jackson Road, Duncan V9L 4W4
(604) 746-4637
Moderate to Expensive

Call for reservations and directions to the Farm.

Fairburn Farm Country Manor has one of the most picture-perfect settings I have seen. The cow-field-type impressions I've had about farms will never be the same. As the innkeeper toured me around, I found myself staring off, unable to concentrate on anything but the scenery of rolling green hills, flawless forested grounds, sweeping fields and gardens of floral brilliance.

After all of that, unfortunately, the bed & breakfast accommodations were a bit too much on the rustic side to qualify as romantic getaways. The rooms are really more family oriented and the bathrooms are shared and down the hall. But, on the chance that the restaurant has extra seatings for lunch or dinner, Fairburn Farm is a must for country-food lovers who find themselves near the town of Duncan. Most of the food is produced on the farm, including the lamb and veal, and the rare treats like fresh-churned butter, stone-ground bread, real maple syrup and homemade jams soothe and satisfy in a way store-bought fare never can.

PINE LODGE FARM
BED & BREAKFAST

3191 Mutter Road, Mill Bay V0R 2P0
(604) 743-4083
Reasonable

Call for reservations and directions to the Farm.

The Pine Lodge Farm is not your typical bed & breakfast, so for an atypical, loving respite this will assuredly fit the need. A 25-mile pilgrimage north of Victoria will place you here, in a serene countryside encompassed by quiet. This eight-bedroom manor has an impressive, staunch, white-pine exterior with an interior that is equally fascinating in its handsome detail and presence. A spacious sitting-room with a large stone fireplace is outlined above by an inside balcony on the second floor, where the guest rooms are situated. The rooms are outfitted with antiques of superior workmanship and design. Each suite can prove a nurturing hide-out, but the rooms with a view of the fields, Strait of Georgia and islands are ideal. Speaking of nurturing, breakfast is a last-you-all-day enterprise prepared with fresh eggs and homemade preserves, so be ready with an appetite to match.

DEER LODGE

R.R. 1, Mill Bay V0R 2P0
(604) 743-2423
Very Inexpensive

Just north of Mill Bay right on Highway 1 on the east side of the road.

This is one of those places I almost passed up because I tend to assume that anything too near a main road or highway isn't romantic. And for the most part that's true, but not at Deer Lodge. In fact, if I were giving awards for the best bargain place to kiss, besides the out-of-doors, Deer Lodge would win hands down. This isn't a fancy renovation, nor are there any four-color brochures to extol the Lodge's character and value. According to the innkeeper, people just keep coming back. I'm certain the return rate is due in part to the enchanting views from the grand bay windows that open out to the water and mainland. It is also due to the generous-sized, cushy suites, most with fireplaces and all with complete kitchens. The units are set facing away from the road, with a manicured lawn and gardens sweeping down the hillside to the view just beyond. This location is one I consider a prize because Vancouver Island can be as expensive as it is beautiful. At Deer Lodge, you can have the beauty without the expense, in easygoing style and comfort.

♦ **ROMANTIC OPTION: The Dutch Latch Restaurant, P.O. Box 26, Malahat V0R 2L0, (604) 478-1880** (Moderate to Expensive), is just down the road a bit from Deer Lodge and you'd think it would also suffer from being right on Highway 1. Yet inside, this is an adorable restaurant with a wonderful wood-framed fireplace, charming country design and tasteful touches all around — and even that isn't the reason to stop here. The Dutch Latch simply has one of the most commanding views of the island's east coast to be found, and the proof is apparent the moment you enter. Best to come during off-hours for dessert or a snack; this is a well-touristed feature along the coast.

VICTORIA

Victoria is accessible by ferryboat from Seattle, Anacortes and Port Angeles in Washington state and from Tsawwassen Bay, Horseshoe Bay and Powell River on the mainland of British Columbia. From Seattle the three direct crossings are the Princess Marguerite (4 1/2 hours one way), the Island Princess (4 1/2 hours one way) and the Victoria Clipper (2 1/2 hours one way). All three take you directly to downtown Victoria.

As much as possible in this book, tourist draws have not been included as best places to kiss — until now, that is. Without question, Victoria is a sprawling tourist center. The famous Empress Hotel, Parliament buildings, Butchart Gardens, historical museums and a wax museum, restaurants and British-fashioned shops, all bordered by a thriving harbor and marina, make the city an attraction-seeker's Nirvana. As a result, especially in summer, it gets very crowded and that is hardly romantic. Yet, Victoria's charisma is hard to ignore. This traditional British town, particularly off-season, can be wonderful. It may even make you feel lustfully regal.

THE BEACONSFIELD

998 Humboldt Street, Victoria V8V 2Z8
(604) 384-4044
Very Expensive

ABIGAIL'S

906 McClure Street, Victoria V8V 3E7
(604) 388-5363
Very Expensive

From the downtown ferry dock, walk toward the Empress Hotel. The street that borders the south side of the hotel is Humboldt. Go east on Humboldt for five blocks; The Beaconsfield is at the intersection of Vancouver and Humboldt streets. To find Abigail's, head two blocks north of The Beaconsfield on Vancouver Street and turn left onto McClure.

The past seems to allow the heart a certain retreat from the stress and strain of modern times. There are many ways to experience the pace of days gone by. One way is to travel the mountains, where civilization hasn't taken root; another is to sojourn to The Beaconsfield or Abigail's and slip into dreamy, sophisticated comfort.

I've listed The Beaconsfield and Abigail's together for three reasons: First, they are owned by the same people; second, they are both dazzling examples of the bed & breakfast experience; and last, they are simply the finest accommodations in Victoria. Every nuance of living in luxury has been seen to and perfected. There is only one problem — deciding whether or not spending time in such sumptuous surroundings is worth the financial splurge.

Abigail's is a classic tudor mansion renovated into a modern inn, finished in pastel shades of rose and green; The Beaconsfield is an Edwardian estate restored to its original look and feel. Essentially, both have rooms designed with only one thing in mind, romance and guiltless pampering. Private Jacuzzis near wood-burning fireplaces . . . plush, richly colored carpeting . . . authentic wash stands . . . winding wood staircases . . . thick goose-down comforters and a generous, gracious breakfast. Of course, the more expensive rooms are the more incredible, but they are really worth it. If you have a special occasion to celebrate, or can create one, either of these bed & breakfasts would be an ideal place for the celebration.

THE CAPTAIN'S PALACE RESTAURANT AND BED & BREAKFAST   💋💋💋💋

309 Belleville Street, Victoria V8V 1X2
(604) 388-9191
Expensive

Across the street from the Princess Marguerite ferry dock and to the left you will see Heritage Village. Next to the Village is the Captain's Palace.

If you haven't already gotten your fill of Victorian heritage, the Captain's Palace is yet another turn-of-the-century replica to venture into for tea, dessert or a snack. The pomp and flourishes of the interior are an indulgent setting for a quiet tete-a-tete or an overnight escapade. In the restaurant, stained glass windows, frescoed ceilings, stately marble and wood fireplaces, crystal chandeliers, antique furnishings and a sweeping stairway with a carved bannister are the lavish appointments that backdrop sherry sipping or an attentively served breakfast and tea. The rooms are Victorian and decorated appropriately with claw-footed bathtubs, cushy beds and outside private balconies. The newer suites, located on the adjacent property, are particularly wonderful and spacious. In short, this convenient-to-everything residence would be a welcome place to return to after a day of walking and sight-seeing in Victoria.

ROMANTIC WARNING: The Captain's Palace restaurant is expensive and the food there isn't as good as at other, less-ornate places in town. If you're not staying there, consider a light snack, tea or wine off-hours to enjoy the setting and service and then continue on to one of the other locations for dinner, like the one in the following romantic suggestion.

♦ *ROMANTIC SUGGESTION:* **Larousse, 1619 Store Street, Victoria, V8V 1W2, (604) 388-4255** (Moderate to Expensive), offers one of the finest dining experiences in Victoria and there is style here to match the sustenance. The ambience is subtle and refined, radiating a simple European charm, and the food is prepared with finesse and the freshest ingredients possible. There are memorable specialties every night — special mousses or salmon complemented with a smooth, piquant sauce, and the vegetable side dishes are as pretty as they are tasty. The desserts are always too good to pass up. Larousse will be a unique, gourmet affair to remember.

HOLLAND HOUSE

595 Michigan Street, Victoria V8V 1S7
(604) 384-6644
Expensive to Very Expensive

From the Princess Marguerite ferry dock, walk toward the Empress Hotel. The street that runs in front of the hotel, on its west side, is Government Street. Heading south, stay on Government till you reach Michigan Street. Holland House is on the corner of Michigan and Government.

From the outside there is little hint of the gorgeous, superior comfort that awaits inside this truly continental-styled inn. From the quaint dining room where a gourmet breakfast is served every morning, to the beautifully furnished rooms and suites, all with elegant baths, some with fireplaces, you will be in designer heaven wherever you find yourselves at the Holland House. An added touch of excellence is the owner's brilliant modern art collection that fills the home with a striking and unique presence. Surely, without sounding too stuffy about it, there isn't a more tasteful inn to be found anywhere.

NOTE: Off-season there are special excursion packages with the Victoria Clipper from Seattle that include the Holland House at bargain prices.

THE ALHAMBRA HOTEL

1140 Government Street, Victoria V8W 1Y2
(604) 384-6835
Expensive to Very Expensive

The hotel is three blocks north of the Empress Hotel on Government Street.

The Alhambra is no ordinary large hotel. It has all the trappings of one, like room service, luggage handlers, a reception desk and yes, even elevators, but there the similarities stop and the heart-stirring differences begin. The rooms are striking and modern in tones of forest green and burgundy and the bathrooms were built for two people to enjoy together. Some of the rooms have huge, tiled shower stalls with two jets; others have Jacuzzis and still others have fireplaces, and then there are a few that have everything, including a view of the inner harbor. Added to all that is a fine complimentary breakfast at the hotel's mezzanine-level restaurant. For an uptown getaway, the Alhambra would fit your requirements and then some.

MOUNT DOUGLAS PARK

From Highway 17, five miles north of downtown Victoria exit to the east on Cordova Bay Road. Follow this road south to the Park.

Minutes away from the center of Victoria is a 500-acre rain forest on the ocean's edge ages away from the tourists and the city. The primal, towering forest, Haro Strait with its island-dotted visage and a winding stretch of beach are all here in utter quiet and solitude. Hike out to your own picnic spot or find your way down to the water, where the view will entertain you for hours on end. After a day or two of Victoria, Mount Douglas Park will be a necessary rest for your senses and spirit.

♦ *ROMANTIC SUGGESTION:* After a day of losing yourselves in Mount Douglas Park, before you venture back to Victoria, stop at the **Cordova Seaview Inn, 5109 Cordova Bay Road, Victoria V8Y 2K1, (604) 658-5227** (Moderate), and relax on the cliff-side patio, where you'll have a bird's-eye view of the wild and peaceful landscape you were just romping through.

SOOKE HARBOR HOUSE

1528 Whiffen Spit Road, Sooke V0S 1N0
(604) 642-3421
Moderate to Very, Very Expensive

The Trans-Canada Highway going west out of Victoria intersects with Highway 14. Take Highway 14 to the town of Sooke about 25 miles northwest of Victoria. The highway goes directly through town. On the north side of town, on the highway, you will see signs for the Sooke Harbor House. At Whiffen Spit Road, turn left. The road dead-ends at the House.

Of all the places I included in the first edition of **Best Places To Kiss,** the Sooke Harbor House has undergone one of the most extensive and fabulous renovations. The original outstanding restaurant remains so, the only exception being that the kitchen, if it's possible, is better than ever. But regarding the bed & breakfast, what was before an okay B&B is now sensational, with the addition of brand-new accommodations in a recently developed building next door. In fact, to call these sensational is actually an understatement.

The restaurant is housed in a two-story country house. When you enter the house you instantly feel the sun's warmth pouring into the dining area from the windows facing the harbor. The rooms above the restaurant are unpretentious, comfortable and reasonably priced. If you decide on the new premium, more deluxe rooms you will find yourselves in luxury the type of which dreams are made. Each one is different, with a combination of hot tub, fireplace, sunken living room and vaulted ceiling, and all have beautiful furnishings. These rooms will be hard to leave, even for breakfast, so be prepared for a weekend that will linger as one of the unforgettable ones you have shared.

♦ **ROMANTIC SUGGESTION:** For either a simple morning hike or a rugged all-day jaunt, **East Sooke Regional Park** provides 3,500 acres of wilderness setting with phenomenal views and trails winding through beautiful beaches and ideal forest.

HOUSE ON THE BAY

7954 West Coast Road, RR 4, Sooke VOS 1N0
(604) 642-6534
Expensive

Call for reservations and directions to the House.

As wonderful as Sooke Harbor House is, it is also expensive. For price and comfort it can't hold a candle to the House On The Bay: a three-acre estate, resting atop a steep cliff overlooking a truly expansive view of the Strait of Juan de Fuca and the mountains on the Olympic Peninsula across the water. The home is designed on two levels with cathedral cedar ceilings and lofty windows that allow the hallowed outside to become an integral part of the inside.

The two suites on the lower floor are spacious and incredibly comfortable. Each one has a private entrance and patio with a far-reaching view, individually designed Japanese-style soak tubs (sans Jacuzzi jets) built for two, kimonos for after your bath, broad showers, queen-size beds, armchairs and Ichiban fresh floral arrangements throughout the year. The decor is a bit on the tacky side but you'll be so relaxed and pampered you won't notice. The breakfast is equal to the accommodations and is your choice of juice, any egg-style you want, homemade croissants, cereals and fresh coffee — all served to you in your room. The House On The Bay is a total package, with all the trimmings you'll need. You even have the restaurant at Sooke Harbor House only 10 minutes away, and the beach is only a short hike from your front door.

MARGISON TEA HOUSE

6605 Sooke Road, Sooke V0S 1N0
(604) 642-3620
Inexpensive

In the town of Sooke, off of Highway 14, 25 miles northwest of Victoria.
As you enter Sooke on Highway 14, watch for a sign indicating the driveway
entrance to the House.

All the out-of-style words and ideas about love and romance —
courting, billing and cooing, turtle-doving, spooning and wooing —
were part of a traditional method of winning a kiss from someone
you loved. Though at first blush it may seem a little too corny or
restrictive, in its own way, old-fashioned can be endearing and fun.

Afternoon tea is a very provincial and proper English thing.
Tablecloth in place, fine china, steaming aromatic tea in silver
service, finger sandwiches and cakes are all integral to tea-time. For
centuries, proposals of all sorts occurred during this late afternoon
ritual. While passing through this amorous countryside, take the time
to do what the natives do: Sip some tea, have a scone or some
Devonshire cream and come up with some proposals of your own.

CHINA BEACH/FRENCH BEACH

Follow Highway 14 past Sooke. You will see a sign 10 miles down the road for French Beach. Further along on Highway 14, one mile past the Jordan River, look for the China Beach sign. China Beach is accessible by a 15-minute walk through rain forest. French Beach is reached by a short, tree-lined path down to the shore.

These two beaches are separated by a few miles and yet are totally connected by their similar settings and rugged character. You can ramble through young, replanted forests or formidable groves of ancient trees or along white sandy beaches forever in either direction. Sure-footedness is a prerequisite though, for you will occasionally have to renegotiate your path over projecting headlands of rocky coast and woods. At either location, you can bask in solitary freedom while being lulled by the water-music on the shore. Visually, cinematic drama is abundant along this relatively undiscovered coastline just a short jaunt from the bustling town of Victoria.

POINT NO POINT RESORT

West Coast Road, Sooke VOS 1N0
(604) 646-2020
Moderate

Forty miles northwest of Victoria, from Highway 14, watch the west side
of the road for a small sign for Point No Point.

Calling these remote cabins a resort is truly inappropriate, for there
is nothing resort-like here. Rather you are dwelling in an area graced
by pure rugged beauty and seemingly eons away from civilization.
Regardless of the weather or time of year, the isolation of this place
spells romance.

The simple rustic cabins with fireplaces, and the rooms in an
adjacent building, rest on the edge of a cliff overlooking a crashing
granite shoreline. Trails with foliage-covered stone archways lead
down to a nearby inlet and small beach. The 11 cabins have large
picture windows facing the water, revealing an unobstructed view of
the ocean and Olympic mountains. Even on a cloud-veiled day, Point
No Point is a bejeweled place softened by the muted colors of ocean
and forest.

NOTE: There are a limited number of cabins and rooms available
here and they book weeks, if not months, in advance.

THE GULF ISLANDS

The Gulf Islands are nestled between Vancouver Island and mainland British Columbia. They lie on the sheltered lee-side of Vancouver Island, constellation-like, up and down the coast. There are over 300 forested isles, whose populations vary from a few hundred to several thousand. Although similar in appearance to the San Juan Islands of Washington state, the Gulf Islands are much less touristed and congested, even during the summer. They are transcendent places of splendor and solitude.

A handful of the Gulf Islands are accessible by ferryboat and each of these has what's required to give you a hassle-free, all-absorbing time away from everything, except nature and each other. Regardless of which island you choose, you will be certain to find oceanfront parks with sweeping views of the other islands, bed & breakfasts set on hilltops or hidden in the woods, unique restaurants where leisurely is a way of life and miles of meandering paved roads leading to island privacy. Whichever island you choose to visit, there will be just two things stealing your gaze: the out-of-this-world scenery and the eyes of the person you love.

FERNHILL LODGE

Box 140, Mayne Island V0N 2J0
(604) 539-2544
Moderate

Call for reservations and directions to the Lodge.

This place is a food-lovers' must. Besides being an uncommonly romantic and affordable bed & breakfast, the Fernhill Lodge also serves a dinner that is a totally exotic dining experience. Until you see this feast firsthand, you will not be able to imagine something like this exists in the countryside of a remote island, or exists at all. Julia Child would be envious of the chef's nightly creations. And "creations" is an over-simplification.

On any given night between May and October you will find two different four-course meals: a farmhouse dinner and a historical-theme dinner. The farmhouse dinners are likely to include jalapeno hush-puppies, red caviar and black pasta, partridge with cherry sauce and chocolate crepes. The historical menu reads almost as splendidly as it tastes: snails in Ethiopian cumin sauce, stuffed dates, Baian oyster stew and wildflower cheesecake. Fabulous! When dinner is done you can retire to your country suite, which overlooks the extensive garden and hillside, and is decorated in one of four period themes from the past. An overnight adventure at the Fernhill Lodge will be a rapturous stay for your hearts and your taste buds.

LA BERENGERIE RESTAURANT AND BED & BREAKFAST

Montague Harbor Road, Galiano Island V0Q 1P0
(604) 539-5392
Reasonable to Moderate

Call for reservations and directions.

Galiano Island is a long, peaceful island with acres upon acres of vigorous forest and gorgeous shoreline. For all intents and purposes, the only reason to come here is to hide from the world for a period of time, filling yourselves up on being close and enjoying nature and quiet, the likes of which you've never heard before. So you wouldn't necessarily expect to find here an authentic French restaurant requiring knowledgeable palates and eager stomachs. Yet La Berengerie is just that, a wonderful restaurant tucked away in the woods of remote Galiano Island. Upstairs from the dining room are three quaint guest rooms, bed & breakfast style, that are comfortable and pretty. The morning meal is an extension of the service and quality you get at night. Because there aren't many charming overnight options on this island, thank goodness La Berengerie is one that fills the bill nicely.

♦ **ROMANTIC OPTION: Holloway House Bed & Breakfast, Burrill Road, Galiano Island, B.C. V0N 1P0, (604) 539-2581** (Moderate), is an authentic log-cabin home with a formidable soapstone fireplace at its center. The majestic ocean-view, country setting, gourmet breakfasts and spacious, cozy rooms with private baths make this unquestionably the other best place for nuzzling and cherishing on Galiano Island.

CLIFFSIDE INN

Armadale Road, North Pender Island V0N 2M0
(604) 629-6691
Reasonable

From the Otter Bay ferry terminal follow all highway signs indicating Hope Bay. At the Hope Bay dock, take Clam Bay Road 1/2-mile east to Armadale Road. Turn north and proceed 600 feet to Cliffside.

A romantic requirement for any holiday is to travel to an awe-inspiring place and, once you arrive, not travel anywhere else for anything. This way you can enjoy an uninterrupted passage of precious time united in relaxation and cuddling. Ferrying to Pender Island will grant you awesome scenery and seclusion, and the Cliffside Inn guarantees the cozy amenities.

The inn straddles a bluff above three acres of concealed oceanfront with wondrous panoramas that take in Mount Baker and Navy Channel. All the rooms in the bed & breakfast are impeccable designer suites with private decks, sun-filled windows and titillating glimpses of the gardens and ocean. The restaurant is a solarium with more of the entrancing view and is well-known for its supremely fresh meals. Cliffside Inn has every romantic requirement for arriving and staying together in undisturbed privacy and serenity.

HASTINGS HOUSE

Box 1110, Ganges, Salt Spring Island V0S 1E0
(604) 537-2362; toll free 1 (800) 661-9255
Expensive to *Unbelievably* Expensive

Take the ferryboat from any of the islands to Long Harbor. Follow the
signs on Long Harbor Road to the town of Ganges, heading west. Turn
south on Robinson Road; watch for the signs that direct you to the House.

Hastings House is doubtless a sparkling gem of a country inn, poised
over Ganges Harbor and the rolling hills of Salt Spring Island.
Everything about this place will tug at your heart-strings, imploring
you to stay longer and luxuriate in the discriminating service and
distinguished renovated buildings of this idyllic 30-acre seaside estate.
Unfortunately, Hastings House will also pull at your purse strings, to
the tune of $160.00 per night (off-season) for a simple sitting room,
on up to $330.00 (high season) for a two story suite with a classic
stone fireplace, two bathrooms and personalized afternoon-tea
service. Every morning before your full-course breakfast is served in
the fireplace-warmed cottage dining room, a basket of fresh pastries
and hot coffee are delivered to your door. As the House's brochure
clearly states, "Meticulous attention is given to character, courtesy,
comfort, calm and cuisine."

Hastings House has to be one of the most expensive, exclusive
places to stay on the West Coast of Canada or the Northwestern
States. If the price is a little over your holiday budget and you want
just a taste of what this type of regal living is like, try their country
restaurant, which serves sumptuous, tantalizing gourmet fare.

◆ **ROMANTIC OPTION:** For those who prefer less pretentious,
less dear accommodations while trysting around Salt Spring Island,
but still want a place that is exceptional, a definite option is
**Southdown Farm Bed & Breakfast, 1121 Beaver Point Road, R.R.
#1, Fulford Harbour, V0S 1C0, (604) 653-4322** (Reasonable to
Moderate). There are two suites on this farm estate: One is a spacious

ground-floor unit of the main house that has an attached conservatory sitting room, and the other is a very private sunlit cottage. Both have Jacuzzis, wood stoves, thick down comforters and lovely interiors. Breakfast is a wonderful occasion with farm-fresh eggs, juice and pastries, and will assuage your appetites well until dinnertime.

"As usual with most lovers in the city
— they were troubled by the lack of that
essential need of love — a meeting
place."

Thomas Wolfe

THE SUNSHINE COAST

The above listing is alphabetical, the descriptions that follow are arranged south to north.

THE SUNSHINE COAST

It might seem odd for a part of the gray, rainy Canadian Southwest to be referred to as *sunshine,* yet, once you travel this section of the world, you'll find a more applicable term doesn't exist. The Sunshine Coast provides all the wonderful rugged sights and sounds you could want and some other getaway opportunities you didn't think existed. Thus, Sunshine in this area means many things bright and beautiful, regardless of weather conditions. Even in the mist of a proverbial foggy morning, the coast is magic.

The Sunshine Coast is a geographically unique location. You will feel like you've tumbled accidentally upon a remote, lengthy peninsula or a long skinny island, and yet it is neither. This section of Canada, beginning at the Gibson's ferry dock and ending at Earl's Cove, is indeed part of the mainland, but because of the water that borders the north, south and west shores and the mountainous eastern border, it is accessible mainly by ferryboat from Horseshoe Bay, northwest of Vancouver. And even though the ferryboat from Horseshoe Bay may seem packed, particularly on a summer day, and you may have to wait awhile to disembark, the other cars will seem to magically melt away as you head north along the coast. It is unlikely you will have a sense of crowds again until you return to the mainland.

ROMANTIC WARNING: The accommodations and most of the restaurants along the Sunshine Coast are best described as mediocre and are not even vaguely romantic. This is almost exclusively RV, camping and boating heaven. There are indeed places to stay and eat but they are not of the same caliber as those found on Vancouver Island. The reason to come here is so the both of you can enjoy the isolation and incredible scenery available at every turn.

HIGHWAY 101

Just past West Vancouver on Highway 99 is Horseshoe Bay. This is a major port for several ferryboat crossings. Follow the signs and schedule for Langdale. Sailing time: 40 minutes. At Langdale, slowly follow Highway 101 north until you reach the end of the road at the ferry dock near Earl's Cove.

The sightseeing along the Sunshine Coast begins the moment the ferryboat leaves Horseshoe Bay. The exhibition starts with mountains that reach down to shore's edge, met by hundreds of variously sized, forested islands checkerboarding the water. In the distance, to the west, Vancouver Island dominates the horizon.

Once you land and continue your drive north, the varying patterns of islands and twisting rocky cliffs parallel to the road, form a grand presentation of the kind this vacationland is known for. Another option for taking in the view is to go by water. There are several charter companies that provide excursions along the coastline, following it faithfully all the way north. But whether from the water or the road, this is one shining place to get away from the rest of the world.

ROMANTIC WARNING: The many coves and inlets along the Malaspine Strait to the west and the Strait of Georgia to the south are obscured from the road for the first 25 miles as you drive from Langdale north to Earl's Cove. Stay patient, the view finally opens and it will be worth the wait. Also, be on the lookout for signs that mark the routes to secluded, out-of-the-way coves lining the water.

♦ **ROMANTIC SUGGESTION:** Before you start your travels north, you may want to muse over your plans together with a snack or meal at the **Mariner's Restaurant, 1500 Marine Drive, Gibson V0N 2W0, (604) 886-2334** (Moderate), in the town of Gibson a few miles north of the Langdale ferry dock. The small, attractive restaurant sits on a bluff overlooking the water. Here there is wonderful visual preparation for the sights yet to come.

CREEK HOUSE

Robert's Creek Road, Robert's Creek V0N 2W0
(604) 885-9321
Expensive

Ten miles north of the Langdale ferry dock on Highway 101, you will find
the turnoff for the town of Robert's Creek. The Creek House restaurant
is in the tiny town, across from the general store and post office.

French country-kitchen dining has a romantic flair all its own. In
part that is due to the blend of elegance accented with rural simplicity.
At the Creek House, the relaxed, cordial ambience of a simply
adorned dining room heated by a stone fireplace and the gourmet-qual-
ity French cuisine are more than any two hearts can endure without
succumbing to the tenderness the scene encourages.

◆ **ROMANTIC SUGGESTION:** After dinner, take a walk or
drive to **Robert's Creek Park** and behold a sunset that will be a
well-designed ending to a gratifying day.

COUNTRY COTTAGE
BED & BREAKFAST

General Delivery, Robert's Creek V0N 2W0
(604) 885-7448
Inexpensive to Moderate

Call for reservations and exact directions to the Country Cottage.

Just up the street from the Creek House is a perfect country alternative to almost any accommodation on this coast. It is one of the only bed & breakfasts on the Sunshine Coast and it is assuredly the only one with any concern for heart-warming atmosphere. Unfortunately there are only two rooms available, and really only one is conducive to intimacy: the cabin adjacent to the main house. It is comfortable and very private and very much for the couple who like to be away from everything.

Breakfast is served in the kitchen to the sound of the wood-burning stove crackling in the background. The sheep, hen house and rambling rose gardens can be part of your morning stroll as you sip coffee and wait for your farm-fresh breakfast to be served. After your hearty morning meal the rest of the day can be spent lounging or searching out the area's adventures.

WAKEFIELD INN

Box 490, Sechelt V0N 3A0
(604) 885-7666
Inexpensive

Follow Highway 101 from the Langdale ferry dock for 20 miles toward
Sechelt. Watch the west side of the road for a large log cabin which is the
Inn. The parking lot is an immediate turn off the highway.

A pub atmosphere generally is not romantic. Pubs tend to be
crowded and encourage beer guzzling, football watching, dart
throwing and political discussions, all of which have their place, but
not in a cuddlesome outing. Nevertheless, this inn is one of the most
charming pit stops you'll ever run into.

At the Wakefield Inn you will feel transported to the Irish
heartland. A bit of that world will greet you in the candescence of
the stone fireplace, a 180-degree view of an island-dotted Sound and
a pathway down to the water. This is an offbeat place to visit after
the visually glorious ferryboat ride. On second thought, there can be
something charming about a tankard of ale and a game of darts before
you start your wanderings through the huge outdoor playground that
is the Sunshine Coast.

ROMANTIC WARNING: Wakefield proclaims itself to be a bed
& breakfast, and technically I guess it is. But the rooms above the
pub are depressing, with a single old lamp, a musty smell, mattresses
whose springs have seen better days, paper-thin walls and a shared
dingy bathroom in desperate need of renovation.

BELLA BEACH MOTEL AND
THE WHARF RESTAURANT

Davis Bay, Sechelt V0N 3A0
(604) 885-7191
Moderate

Twenty-five miles north of the ferry dock at Langdale, just south of Sechelt off Highway 101, on the east side of the road.

As I've mentioned, there isn't much in the way of romantic accommodations on the Sunshine Coast, unless you bring your own tent for the many lovely campgrounds that line the beaches and bays. But if roughing it isn't your idea of romance, the Bella Beach Motel is one of your better options. Its large, comfortable rooms face the vast ocean with Vancouver Island looming in the distance. One slight drawback is that the main road lies between the motel and the water. Still, the view is one you can be engaged with for hours and the traffic is never all that heavy, so the highway doesn't get in the way as much as you'd think.

The beach across the road and accessibility to the entire coast make this a worthwhile place to use as a home base while you explore the coast. You will also be pleased that right next to Bella Beach is The Wharf Restaurant. Breakfast and lunch are reasonably priced, the food creative and tasty and the ambience cozy and attractive.

SECRET COVE

Follow Highway 101 ten miles past Sechelt to Secret Cove. The highway will turn off to an unpaved road, which ends at a parking area. From the parking lot, a short hike will take you out to the cove.

This is one of the coast's dozens of watery enclaves that are both spectacular and isolated. After meandering a short distance through rain forest, you will be exposed to a view that is provocative in any weather. A sunny day reveals an entirely private inlet, etched from the finest assortment of rocky, jagged coastal formations. In the overcast opaqueness of a fall/winter day, you may imagine an English seaside filtering through the clouds. To indulge in this international fantasy, don't forget to pack scones and a thermos filled with tea to snack on when you stop at your destination. If by chance you hear some strange sounds emanating from the water or islands, don't be surprised. You've probably just happened upon a group of playful sea lions or otters frolicking in the afternoon sun or evening tides.

NOTE: Take the time to charter a boat from one of the many local marinas, or take one of the lunch or dinner cruises through the exquisite water byways. You will have enviable stories to tell once you get home. Well, at least the parts you can share.

Skookumchuck Narrows

Drive north on Highway 101 about 60 miles, following the signs to the ferryboat at Earl's Cove. Just before reaching the dock, you will see signs for Egmont and the Narrows. Turn east and follow the road to the parking area. A quarter-mile hike will take you out to the Narrows.

The Canadian Southwest and the Pacific Northwest are filled with more than enough natural wonders to satisfy the most jaded world traveler. Skookumchuck Narrows is one particularly intriguing wonder. The enormous energy generated by this spectacle is so moving (figuratively and literally), no words can really describe the resulting feelings it can trigger.

The trail out to the Narrows is endowed with abundant foliage — ground carpeted in autumn-colored leaves and trees wrapped in leis of moss. As you make your way out to the tip of this peninsula, you'll approach Sechelt Inlet on the east side. You can stand almost next to the edge of the rock-bordered passage that is the gateway to this body of water. Through this tiny portal, at high or low tide, the rush of water is so intense that the land actually shakes beneath your feet. You can feel this vibration throughout your body, from the sheer force of the daily tidal exchange. This is the time and place where, without even kissing or touching, you can really feel the earth move.

FERRYBOAT RIDE FROM EARL'S
COVE TO SALTERY BAY

From the ferry dock at Langdale follow the signs on Highway 101 to Earl's Cove at the northern end of the highway. Be sure to check the scheduled ferry crossings from Earl's Cove.

If you don't have a chance to become acquainted with the Sunshine Coast from either your own boat or a chartered boat trip, then the ferry crossing from Earl's Cove to Saltery Bay is a must. The passage affords a rare opportunity to partake in the marine enchantment this area is famous for.

There is an array of snow-capped mountains that frame your tour through the Jervis Inlet. The forested, rocky mainland-projections down to the water are magnificent. Depending on the season, be on the watch for whales as the ferry makes its way around and through this watery highway. This is one of their homes during the late winter and early spring, and they can perform at the most unexpected times of day, making this excursion feel like a momentary romp with nature.

SCENE-HOPPING RECOMMENDATION: Start out at the **Wakefield Inn** or the **Mariner's Restaurant** for breakfast, then head out to **Skookumchuck Narrows** for a quick day-hike, being sure to check the tide schedule before you go. A salmon barbecue lunch-cruise from the **Sunshine Coast Tours & Charters** can take you along the thrilling coast for a relaxing few hours. Then, after a leisurely walk along one of the many coves, you can finish with dinner at the **Creek House Restaurant.**

> *"To write a good love letter, you ought to begin without knowing what you mean to say and to finish without knowing what you have written."*
>
> Jean Jacques Rousseau

W H I S T L E R

The above list is alphabetical. The following descriptions are arranged from south to north.

WHISTLER

Whistler and Blackcomb mountains are world famous for their fabulous skiing — though during any season, the entire area is a mountain-lover's Mecca. Whistler's raison d'etre is the enjoyment of every aspect of outdoor recreation you could possibly fathom: downhill, cross-country and helicopter skiing; kayaking, canoeing, wind surfing and white-water rafting; hiking, mountain biking and golfing. All these activities are available near Whistler Village, an international-styled ski development alive with restaurants, shops and lodging. If you like high-paced fun and a party atmosphere amid purple mountain majesty, Whistler delivers in the slickest, most impressive way possible.

The only drawback to this mountainous playing field is that the town of Whistler is growing so fast and there is so much building taking place, the area is beginning to resemble a suburban con-dominium sprawl — convenient for skiing and very social, but not necessarily intriguing or charming. Don't be too concerned about any of that; with the suggestions that follow, Whistler's impersonal facade can quickly melt into romantic sparkle and secret solitude.

NOTE: Alternative times to sojourn here are summer and fall — well before the first snowfall, like a pied piper's song, beckons the skiers to the slopes. Besides, during the summer there is still glacier skiing available at the very top of both Blackcomb and Whistler mountains. It's not the mile-long runs of the winter season, but then again, in the winter you can't wear your bathing suit down the slopes.

HIGHWAY 99

From Vancouver cross into West Vancouver via Highway 1 north over the Second Narrows Bridge or Highway 1/99 over the Lion's Gate Bridge. Follow the signs to Squamish and Whistler. Depending on the road conditions, this is about an hour-and-a-half drive.

There is nothing quite like this landscape's combination of rock, forest, snowcapped peaks and water all converging together to stimulate and flood the senses. The perilous drop of cliffs, the cerulean flow of mountain waterways, dramatic waterfalls and uninterrupted, fragrant pinery together form the best of all outdoor worlds. The drive along Highway 99, nicknamed the Sea-To-Sky Highway, is so outrageously gorgeous that there is literally relief when a curve takes you away from the view and lets you get your mind back on driving. But that doesn't happen very much during the first half of your trip so be sure to agree together beforehand who's going to drive, or else take turns. Both of you should get a chance to gawk at the labyrinth of wonder that constitutes the 90 miles of curvaceous highway from Vancouver to Whistler. This drive is a sensation not to be missed.

CAUTION: Winter driving conditions can be hazardous.

SHANNON FALLS

North of Vancouver on Highway 99, about halfway to Whistler on the east side of the road. Look for signs that identify Shannon Falls.

Highway turnoff sites are both practical places to stop for momentary respites from the road and great ways to review where you've just been or where you're heading. You don't have to hike anywhere, the big-screen viewing begins the instant you stop. The turnoff to Shannon Falls is a *turnoff lovers'* view extravaganza.

Immediately after you pull off the main road into the parking area and silence the engine, you will hear the thunder of a huge waterfall, plummeting straight down the face of the mountain. One would expect such a spectacle as this to be the reward at the end of a long, arduous trail and not in the middle of a rest area, but here it is nevertheless. Before you leave Vancouver to start your trek up the mountain, be sure to pack a picnic to enjoy at the base of this lofty shower so you can take advantage of a very accessible scenic paradise.

BRANDYWINE FALLS

Take Highway 99 north to Whistler. A few miles before Whistler, you will see signs directing you to the Falls.

A brisk 10-minute walk through lush forest will bring you to a feat of natural construction that deserves a standing ovation: At the end of your jaunt, the pine trees open out to a cliff that looks across to the top of Brandywine Falls.

The water drops forever down a tube-like canyon into the river below, which cuts through a valley of interlacing mountains and meadows. During the summer, you can climb down to the rocky ledges under the falls below and, side by side, sit under the surging waters feeling the spray cool the sun's warmth.

RIMROCK CAFE AND OYSTER BAR

Box 70, Whistler V0N 1B0
(604) 932-5525
Moderate

After you enter the town of Whistler, look for the Highland Lodge just south of the gondola, at the base of Whistler Mountain, on the east side of the road. The restaurant is on the Lodge's second story.

It is difficult for new construction to ever honestly have the ambience of rustic charm. Even when a place is tastefully done, it tends to have a modern quality that is nice but not necessarily engaging. An exception to that rule is the restaurant at the Highland Lodge, unromantically named Rimrock Cafe. Its stone fireplace spans one entire wall, filling the room with a glow that blushes against the wood-paneled walls, the tables and floors.

When it comes to the food, the spectacle is on the plate. The freshest fish is bonded nicely with light sauces and partnered with tender vegetables, all flawlessly prepared and kindly served. After a madcap day of skiing or hiking, or a lazy afternoon communing with nature, this is a handsome hiding place to idle lovingly over dinner and intimate conversation.

THE GABLES

Sea-To-Sky Accommodations, P.O. Box 519, Whistler V0N 1B0
(604) 932-4184

Off-Season/Moderate — Ski-Season/Very Expensive

*Two miles after you enter the town of Whistler on Highway 99, turn into
the Whistler Village just off the Highway. Follow the road straight, passing
the Village, and turn right where it dead-ends. The road curves around
heading toward the Wizard Express ski lift. You will see The Gables on
the west side of the road, just before the lift.*

Besides excellent ski runs and the latest in express chair lifts,
Whistler is filled with condos of every size, shape and price range.
From the heart of the Village to the base of the gondola up to Whistler
Mountain and even farther out on the back roads away from
everything, there are more than enough accommodations to suit every
taste, budget and the hordes of winter enthusiasts. But the one thing
you may find lacking is a place to soothe the heart as well as the
muscles after a day of tackling the slopes. The Gables is a small,
elegant development just a two-minute walk from the Village and
right across the street from the Wizard Express. In spite of this easy
access, these units are surprisingly sedate and beautifully appointed,
a far cry from the typical units prevalent throughout the area.

In each apartment there is a small hallway as you walk in that
nicely handles wet clothing and snow-laden boots. The living room
is then entered through glass-paned french doors. All the units have
fireplaces and fully equipped kitchens, and the bathrooms have
Jacuzzi-jetted bathtubs. In each unit the cozy bedroom upstairs is a
loft overlooking the capacious living room. You can even choose
whether the apartment will have a staggering view of the mountain,
or a soothing view of the rushing creek at the back of the property.
All in all, The Gables' proximity to everything and the inviting
quality of the rooms, make it a fetching place to escape to after a
day's mountainous pursuits.

BLACKCOMB MOUNTAIN SUMMER DINNER

4545 Blackcomb Way, Whistler V0N 1B0
(604) 932-3141
Moderate

Call for reservations and the time for meeting at the Wizard Express ski lift.

It's a shame this dinner excursion, which takes place on top of the world, happens only during the summer. But Whistler's early sunset (about 3:30 pm) during the height of winter season makes this dining event purely a summer fling. It is when the snow — except for the perennial glacial patch at Blackcomb's summit — has melted and sunset seems to linger forever across the face of the mountains that this unbelievable dinner and ride are possible and you learn what a feast in heaven must be like.

You start at the Wizard Express lift, transferring to the Solar Coaster and once more to the 7th Heaven Express. This brings you to the top of Blackcomb, where The Rendezvous restaurant waits with an impressive five-course dinner. As good as the food is, it is still only a minor part of why your evening up here will be miraculous. This dining location is so transcendent it will take a while for your eyes to adjust to the magnitude of the view around you. Even to call this dinner-spectacle the pinnacle of romance is an understatement, but until you venture up here and see it for yourselves, no other phrase says it better.

♦ **ROMANTIC OPTION:** If keeping your feet on the ground in the Village is a preferred dining experience for the two of you, consider an evening at **Myrtle's Restaurant (604) 932-5211** (Expensive) in the Timberline Lodge (see entry for Timberline Lodge). Here the elegant atmosphere and exceptional cuisine make every meal a romantic treat.

TIMBERLINE LODGE

4122 Village Green, Whistler VON 1B0
1 (800) 663-5474
Expensive to Very Expensive

Turn into Whistler Village and follow the signs to Timberline Lodge.

My dear friend Julie, who loves romantic ski-weekends, asked me
to find a cozy, adorable accommodation somewhere in the heart of
Whistler Village. She felt strongly that half the experience of Whistler
was the evening excitement of the town after the slopes were closed.
I felt strongly that the Village had everything you could want for
apres skiing, except romance. But far be it from me to decline a
challenge, so I searched through every inn, lodge and hotel the
Village had to offer and came up with Timberline Lodge. All the
details are here for an oasis of alpine comfort, including a fireplace,
four-poster bed, terrace, wet bar and Jacuzzi in each room. All the
rooms are so unique, you'll need to request a list to figure out which
one will exactly meet your needs; but each is assured to grant the
wishes of a skier's heart.

◆ **ROMANTIC OPTION:** Whistler has several pensiones that
cater to those who want a reclusive, homey environment as well as
a hearty meal first thing in the morning just before the slopes open.
**Chalet Luise Pension (Bed & Breakfast), 7461 Ambassador
Crescent, Box 352, Whistler VON 1B0, (604) 932-4187** (Reasonable to Moderate), has a little bit of everything for those who brave
the mile-long mountain runs: quaint rooms with views and balconies,
an outdoor whirlpool, a fireside lounge and a large breakfast area to
linger in over an ample array of pastry, egg dishes and hot coffee,
plus all the extra comforts you would expect from a European-styled
bed & breakfast.

MEAGER CREEK HOT SPRINGS

*Take Highway 99 north past Whistler to the town of Pemberton. Follow
the signs to Pemberton Meadows. Approximately 15 miles up the road
toward Pemberton Meadows you will see a sign for the Coast Mountain
Outdoor School. At this point, turn right onto Meager Main Line. Stay
on this somewhat treacherous logging road for a bumpy 27 miles. At the
sign for 27 miles, turn left. After you pass an area of felled timber, parking
is a short distance ahead.*

There are only a few kissing places in this book that are a pain to
reach. A pain refers to a drive that is either long, boring, unattractive
or a combination of all three and road conditions that will eat your
car alive. The drive to Meager Hot Springs is one of the *trial-by-fire*
kind of drives because a good deal of the trip is on eroded, active
logging roads. However, if you have an all-terrain vehicle or a car
that can take it, don't let any of that stop you. The dip that awaits
you is unforgettable.

Once you arrive, a short footpath takes you into a maze of
subterranean-heated pools and streams. A steamy mist rises lazily
from the ground, extending to the rocky perimeters of the springs,
and then disappears into the crisp-cool air above. As you bask together
in the warm, soothing water, your attention will be diverted to the
towering features beyond. Or, if a vapory fog envelops you, it will
be easy to imagine you are relaxing in tropic temperatures, in an
ethereal veil of privacy. Hot-tubbing at the health club was never
like this. And talk about private — chances are you will have the
entire place to yourselves, especially during off-season.

NOTE: Because these hot springs are not well-marked and because
this is an active logging road, before starting your trip, inquire at the
visitor's center in Pemberton for all necessary information. Also be
aware that nightfall or snow can create dangerous driving conditions.

TYAX MOUNTAIN LAKE RESORT 👄👄👄

Tyaughton Lake Road, Gold Bridge V0K 1P0
(604) 238-2221
Moderate to Expensive

North of Vancouver on Highway 99, drive through Whistler and Pemberton to the town of Gold Bridge. From the main road in Gold Bridge follow the signs to the resort.

An alpine meadow at the heart of the Canadian Rockies, a crystal clear lake, mountain goats roaming the hillside and eagles soaring overhead — this is the stuff romantic escapes are made of. Include in that picture an imposing log building housing 28 elegant, authentically countrified suites; private cabins; and all the outdoor and indoor adventures you can imagine, and you have described Tyax Resort. It's all true, plus: Three incredible, formal meals are graciously served in the main lodge every day. The bread is baked in a huge stone oven and the freshest food imaginable is deftly combined to satisfy the most discriminating of tastes.

Depending on the package you choose and the time of year you travel, the following are available to assure your outdoor entertainment: snowshoes, skates, toboggans, mountain bikes, ice-fishing equipment, snowmobiles, horseback riding, wind surfing, river rafting, heli-hiking, fishing tours, float-plane fishing, sleigh rides, canoeing, cross-country skiing, tennis, hayrides and an outdoor Jacuzzi. For limitless romantic adventure, absolute privacy and breathtaking surroundings, this unique lodge is a short 110 miles north of Vancouver, in relative obscurity to most Canadians and Americans.

Are Fancy Restaurants Romantic?

Maybe it's my laid-back Northwest attitude that makes me instinctively averse to expensive restaurants where the waiters or other patrons sneer at you if you drop your fork or ask for cold red wine. In terms of romance, the problems with fancy in general are, one, it's hard to be free with your affections when your every move is under scrutiny, and two, formal places tend to require getting dressed up, which tends to discourage intimacy until you get home and undressed.

There is also a notion that dwelling on eating out in fancy restaurants is a major form of romantic activity, but that is not the attitude of this book. Suffice it to say that the restaurants listed here have more to offer than just pricey dinners and chic pastel interiors. Neither is the main point to establish them as great or endearing places to dine; their special quality is that they nurture the heart as they please the palate and satisfy the stomach. There are many ways in which that can be done: mesmerizing views, affectionate cozy interiors, pampering service without snobbery, and, of course, a respectable amount of space between the tables (*like the difference in the space between a subcompact and a sedan*).

Also, note that there are inexpensive ways to enjoy any eating establishment that is over your price range. Consider having your main course at home or at a restaurant more in line with your budget and then enjoy dessert and espresso, to your hearts' and wallets' content, at the dining place of your choice. ALL the restaurants in this book can be a bargain if you know how to order and how not to drink.

THE VANCOUVER AREA

continues

The above listings are arranged alphabetically. The descriptions that follow are loosely arranged from the downtown area heading north.

VANCOUVER

Vancouver has so much to offer and is so geographically beautiful that, for other metropolitan areas, it is a stunning model of a big city done right. From Stanley Park and the Seawall to the nightlife at Gastown, to ethnic restaurants and more ethnic restaurants, lavish hotels, the theatre, discos, nightclubs, the skyline encircling English Bay, the reaches of formal gardens, botanically brilliant conservatories, sophisticated architecture, the three mountains that border the city on the north, and the island-flecked Strait of Georgia, this city is romantically composed and fastidiously maintained.

Here the tremor of urban life is manifest in miles of lights, steel-girded bridges and skyscrapers. The urban landscape embraces pastoral beauty — a symphony of tableaus made up of mountains, parks and ocean. You will be enticed by the vibrant, varied surroundings to seek out the inexhaustible daytime sights or the hot nightlife action.

Yet, regardless of this excitement, or rather because of it, Vancouver itself isn't the place to display your amour. Major metropolitan areas are hard to conceive of as kissable places. What precludes large cities from being classified as such is their populations. It's hard to avoid several-hundred-thousand people, unless you're locked in a hotel room or you've located an obscure park on the outskirts of town, and even then you can't be certain. Of course, none of this means that you should avoid Vancouver, or Seattle or Portland for that matter. Quite the contrary. Simply be cautious and prepare yourselves for a more citified, conventional type of date than what the country and islands have to offer.

NOTE: For more detailed travel guidance while in Canada, consult the information centers scattered generously along most major roads and throughout most towns. These people are so lovely you should stop in just to say hello and get your first taste of Canadian hospitality. For Vancouver information, contact Tourism Vancouver, #1625-1055 West Georgia Street, P.O. Box 11142, Royal Centre, Vancouver V6E 4C8, telephone (604) 682-2222.

THE PROW RESTAURANT

999 Canada Place, Vancouver V6C 3B5
(604) 684-1339
Moderate to Expensive

Canada Place is at the intersection of Howe and Cordova streets on the eastern coastline of downtown, where the cruise ships dock and the Pan Pacific Hotel is located.

Entering this establishment will be an indelible romantic episode in your lives. How can it fail? The dining room overlooks the Burrard Inlet, offset by mountains, glittering city lights and imperious ships forging their way through the water. The interior is dressed in pastel peaches and greens and the tables have room between them to spare. Add to all this a menu that is as virtuous as the view is heart-throbbing and you have a restaurant that far surpasses its touristy location. The fish dishes seem to have jumped from the water to the kitchen and are adorned with oyster mushrooms and light cream sauces that have been carefully cooked. The desserts are bountiful, and well, there's that view again. From the setting to the cuisine, this location is satisfying all the way around.

◆ **ROMANTIC OPTION:** If the Prow Restaurant is crowded you can always relax awhile next door in the **Cascades Lounge at the Pan Pacific Hotel, Canada Place, Vancouver V6C 3B5, 1(800) 663-1515.** This immense, airy, echoing bar lords over the same astonishing view as the Prow, through arresting floor-to-ceiling windows. Not the prettiest of interiors or even vaguely intimate, but with each other and what's outside you'll do just fine until your table opens up at the Prow.

RESTAURANT GERARD

845 Burrard Street, Vancouver V6Z 2K6
1(800) 543-4300
Very Expensive

Located in the Meridien Hotel in downtown Vancouver, on Burrard Street between Smithe and Robson.

Restaurant Gerard is more popularly known as Gerard's, but that is as abbreviated as it gets — you would never think of calling it Gerry's. The very posh and very dignified Restaurant Gerard is located in the very extravagant Meridien Hotel. Be aware that dinner here is not in any way, shape or form a laid-back dining event. Quite the contrary; it is one of those stately, glamorous affairs, where getting dressed to the nines is a must so you can have dinner by 7.

Breakfast at Gerard's can be a rather ordinary affair with a below-average buffet offering. Lunch is very good, but heavily attended by the business crowd. Dinner, on the other hand, provides the framework for culinary excesses and romantic exchanges. If a bit of opulent continental dining is your way of celebrating a new day together, Gerard's is a tour de force for the occasion.

NOTE: The lounge at Restaurant Gerard is a handsome mahogany-paneled room that features intimate corners where privacy is almost always guaranteed.

♦ **ROMANTIC OPTION:** For a less expensive but truly adept French restaurant, venture into the **Chef & The Carpenter on 1745 Robson Street, Vancouver V6E 1G2, (604) 687-2700 (Moderate).** This quaint, intimate dining room and enterprising cuisine will guarantee you a gourmet-romantic meal. Then, after dinner, if the mood seems right, enjoy a snifter of brandy at the aesthetic lounge at Gerard's.

WEST END GUEST HOUSE

1362 Haro Street, Vancouver V6E 1G2
(604) 681-2889
Very Reasonable

Located on Haro Street one block south of Robson Street, between Jervis and Broughton streets.

I'm still not sure why there are so few bed & breakfasts in the Vancouver area; I've been told it has something to do with licensing problems. Though there is a service you can call for B&B-type accommodations, that tends to get you, literally, a bed in someone's home and a 50/50 chance of a comfortable arrangement. So when I tell you about the West End Guest House, don't be surprised if you have difficulty getting reservations there — it's practically the only B&B in town, and, except for its overbright exterior, everything about the place is simply wonderful and endearing.

This *electric-pink,* turn-of-the-century house is a bit startling when you first see it, dwarfed between two large modern apartment buildings in a neighborhood that is almost exclusively high-rises. The outside contrasts with a gentler persona inside, where it has been beautifully restored and decorated in an imaginative blend of practical and whimsical: striking blonde-wood trim, high ceilings, crystal chandeliers, bay windows, soft down quilts, suites that have ample space and private, adorable bathrooms, and a breakfast area with individual wood tables. There are modern conveniences, like televisions and telephones, without the usual sterility. For a romantic change from the ritzy, skyscraper hotels, the West End Guest House is a soothing alternative.

♦ **ROMANTIC OPTION:** If the West End Guest House is booked, the innkeepers there may direct you to **The Barclay Hotel, 1348 Robson Street, Vancouver, V6E 1C5, (604) 688-2534** (Reasonable to Moderate). This is not a bed & breakfast, nor is it totally like a hotel; rather it is more like a European lodging, with appealing, quaint architecture on the outside and cozy, proper rooms on the inside — of the type that face the busy streets of Paris or Brussels — only you are here, on Robson Street, one of the most lively, fashionable shopping districts of the U.S. and Canadian western coasts.

CAFFE DE MEDICI

1025 Robson Street, Vancouver V6E 1C5
(604) 669-9322
Moderate to Expensive

Robson Street is in the downtown section of Vancouver.

Robson Street is a confluence of specialty shops, bakeries, cafes, bistros, superb restaurants and designer boutiques, traveling a 1/2-mile course through downtown. Centered in one of the more swank clusters of shops, away from the bustle of the street, is Caffe de Medici. The character of this restaurant is Northern Italian, artistically composed with colors of forest green and maroon; high, arched ceilings; thick plush drapery. The polished interior is matched by the rich, delicious entrees, service that is flawless and genteel, and an unmistakable romantic atmosphere. On Robson Street the choices for dining out seem unfathomable; Caffe de Medici narrows the field down to one.

THE WEDGEWOOD HOTEL

845 Hornby Street, Vancouver V6Z 1V1
(604) 689-7777
Expensive to Very Expensive

On Hornby Street in downtown Vancouver, between Burrard and Howe.

Of all the formal, gigantic hotels in downtown Vancouver, my favorite is this rather petite exception to the rule, The Wedgewood. Its white french doors open to a concinnate lobby and an elegant, quiet lounge that has not been taken over by the serious business-suit crowd. The rooms are arranged with sitting areas and separate bedrooms, so the feeling is more like an uptown apartment and less like a hotel. There are fireplaces in many of the suites and all of them have foliage-draped decks that help alleviate the claustrophobia high-rises tend to inspire.

NOTE: The Wedgewood dining room is one of the most graceful, demure places in Vancouver for an intimate breakfast, or any meal for that matter. In the winter you will be warmed by the glowing fireplace, in summer you will be cooled by the bright white and green tones of the decor, and throughout the year the well-prepared food will revitalize and please.

THE TEAHOUSE RESTAURANT

Stanley Park on Ferguson Point, Vancouver
(604) 669-3281
Moderate

From the north end of the park turn west off Highway 99 and follow
Stanley Park Drive along the park's western side. Follow the signs to the
Teahouse.

This restaurant is a truly extraordinary kissing place. The only
problem is that it's hard to decide whether it's a tourist attraction or
one of the most beautiful places to dine in all of British Columbia.
A large part of the sparkle comes from the location: The Teahouse
rests in the middle of a sloping lawn overlooking English Bay and,
on the horizon, Vancouver Island. The building itself is dazzling, half
of it a pastel-colored country home and half a glass-enclosed atrium.
Here you can watch the sun gently tuck itself into the ocean for a
peaceful night's rest — that is, if you have reservations or come during
off-hours. Everyone, including the busloads of tourists, knows about
The Teahouse Restaurant. Separate from the scenery, the restaurant
serves fairly standard Canadian-French cuisine that is a tad too
standard and generally over-sauced, but not all the time. The seafood,
egg bakes and meats, when prepared au naturel, can be tasty, so order
carefully. But that view! Sigh, your hearts and eyes will be thankful
for a long time to come.

ROMANTIC WARNING: Stanley Park is a spectacular oasis of
thick forest, green hilly lawns and lakes, with paved trails weaving
through its 1,000 acres of cloistered parkland. The park is almost like
an island, projecting as it does out into the water with English Bay
on one side and Burrard Inlet on the other. From the Seawall
Promenade wrapping around the park, to the zoo, aquarium, picnic
areas galore, the lengthy shoreline at Sunset Beach, vistas and more
vistas, restaurants and lakes, Stanley Park is a veritable refuge from
the cityscape only moments away. Its only problem is the same one

the Teahouse Restaurant has: There isn't much privacy. However, the surroundings are so welcoming, you can forgive the busloads of camera-clicking tourists and find yourselves a corner to call your own — at least for a while.

MARINE DRIVE

Marine Drive follows the southern shoreline of West Vancouver. Heading north over the Lion's Gate Bridge turn west onto Marine Drive.

Marine Drive follows, at water's edge, one of the most fabulous residential neighborhoods in the Vancouver area. Summertime fashions this road with perfect views of the city and Vancouver Island. During the fall, overcast rainy days make this sinuous road more reclusive, emphasizing its dark, rocky cliffs and thick, moist foliage that veils the houses along the way.

Besides being scenic and conducive to sitting close (if you don't have bucket seats), Marine Drive has an added attraction: Several satellite roads leading north off of the drive will connect you with two alternative routes to Whistler: Cypress Access Road through Cypress Provincial Park and Capilano Road over Grouse Mountain. Let the virtue of the drive lead you wherever it compels you to go.

JAPANESE GARDENS

In Vancouver, off Northwest Marine Drive, on the grounds of the University of British Columbia.

Mysterious and captivating are words not often associated with a garden, yet they succinctly describe the imagery and impact of the Japanese Gardens. Coaxed from the earth by skilled artisans, this botanical presentation is creative and authentic: The patterns of delicately sculpted shrubbery are haloed by Oriental-cut trees that bestow the garden with exotic emphasis. Spending a quiet afternoon here will be like visiting another country, without the trouble.

NOTE: There is an entrance fee into the gardens.

GROUSE MOUNTAIN
MOUNT SEYMOUR PROVINCIAL PARK
CYPRESS PROVINCIAL PARK

These mountains are accessible from Highway 1 and Highway 1A/99. To get to Mount Seymour Provincial Park, follow the signs from North Vancouver off of Highway 1 heading east. Cypress Bowl Road in West Vancouver takes you to Cypress Provincial Park. Capilano Road in West Vancouver leads to Grouse Mountain.

One extraordinary aspect of Vancouver is that in its very own back yard there are three separate mountains high enough above sea level to be active ski areas, and they are only about 30 minutes from the city, 45 minutes if you take your time or get lost. It is quite feasible to spend a whimsical day on any of these mountains hiking, lake-swimming (depending on the season), gazing out over the stupendous views or skiing and still have more than enough time to get back to the city and dress up for a candlelit, sumptuous dinner in Gastown at, say, the **Cherrystone Cove Restaurant, 73 Alexander, (604) 681-7020** (Expensive) or **DuBruilles, 745 Thurlow, (604) 681-3818** (Expensive). Don't be surprised if, after you've eaten, there is still an extra hour or two left to return home, kick your shoes off and reminisce about the cherished day you both just shared.

ROMANTIC WARNING: All three areas are well-known but Grouse Mountain tends to be the most touristy of the group.

ROMANTIC SUGGESTION: For the more adventurous couple, on a moonlit winter's eve, consider doing the previous scenario in reverse. After an early dinner in the city, go home, gather your cross-country ski equipment, toss it in the car and drive up to Cypress Provincial Park. Stride over the sparkling-white, luminous snow until the park lights shut off at 11:00 p.m.

LIGHTHOUSE PARK

From Highway 1/99 in West Vancouver, take the 21st Street exit to Marine Drive. Follow the signs on Marine Drive to Lighthouse Park.

The southwestern tip of West Vancouver is a peninsula called Lighthouse Park. It is a small, water-bound fragment of granite hanging on to the mainland. From the parking area, the shores of the Strait of Georgia or the top of the park's cliffs are both only a brisk 15-minute walk over divergent trails through rocky forest. Along any of the trails, you can inhale the freshness of sea air mingling with the scent of sturdy pine trees.

At trail's end, the view from either vantage point, from the top or below, is far-reaching on a clear day. On a cloud-covered day, Lighthouse Park obligingly resembles the kind of rain forest that exists deep in the distant mountains of the Canadian Rockies, enabling you to feel far away from city life. The two of you will scarcely remember how close civilization really is.

◆ **ROMANTIC ALTERNATIVE:** After heading back east on Marine Drive from Lighthouse Park and through the town of West Vancouver, look for a waterfront park called **Ambleside** just west of Lion's Gate Bridge. The long, winding sidewalk that outlines the park is bordered on one side by a stone seawall with marvelous views of the water and city, and on the other by grass and playgrounds. In effect, this is a much smaller, less crowded version of the Seawall in Stanley Park and a definite romantic option if crowds are something you like to avoid.

DEEP COVE

Take Highway 1 through North Vancouver, over the Second Narrows Bridge. Follow the signs for the Mount Seymour Parkway exit heading east. Stay on the Parkway until you come to Deep Cove Road and turn north. The road dead-ends at Deep Cove.

A mountain-ensconced marina, a single rural-style main street relatively untouched by commercialization, and a small, forested park with wooden stairs leading down to the water are the things that describe Deep Cove. The small village of Deep Cove looks out north to Mount Seymour and west to an arcade of mountains separated from the town by a vast body of water called Indian Arm. Deep Cove is so close to Vancouver that it would be easy to engineer a trip out here. The area is a quiet celebration both of nature's ability to create astonishing, enduring scenery and of people's ability to leave it well enough alone.

◆ **ROMANTIC SUGGESTION:** Have dinner or brunch at the **Nutshell Restaurant, 4402 Gallant, Deep Cove, North Vancouver, V7G 1L2, (604) 929-1721** (Expensive), and you will risk being spoiled by an overwhelming view and interesting dining experience that is a cross between the laid-back attitude of the '60s and continental cuisine. You can count on the menu selections to tempt the palate all the time and be successful creations some of the time.

> *"Love is the triumph of imagination over intelligence."*
>
> H.L. Mencken

The places above are listed alphabetically. The descriptions are arranged geographically on the following pages east to west.

PORT TOWNSEND

Port Townsend is the farthest point northeast on the Olympic Peninsula and was originally settled back in the 1800s. The flavor of that time is still reflected in the homes rooted on a bluff overlooking the waterfront parks, shops and restaurants of the town. Tapestry woven sunsets and sunrises of tinted clouds color this provincial setting, accenting the historical quality of its buildings. The dedication to authentic restoration of period architecture is this town's trademark, and every corner has outstanding examples of a past preserved with honor and beauty. Whatever your romantic flair, you are unlikely to leave here disappointed. Port Townsend can easily become a favorite getaway from hectic urban life.

NOTE: Port Townsend is a popular town whose spirit has not succumbed to the flood of summer and weekend tourist traffic. But for more intimacy, avoid the summer crowds and visit early in the week or off-season, during the misty fall and winter.

THE CABIN

839 North Jacob Miller Road, Port Townsend 98368
(206) 385-5571
Reasonable

Call for reservations and directions to The Cabin.

After I describe this consummate kissing location, do not hold it against me that there is only one cabin here and reservations are very hard to come by, especially during the summer. But it happens to be an irresistible, heart-tugging place and the outside setting only makes it more seductive and is what gives it an ultra-secluded allure. The petite log building is impeccably done in a country motif, adorned with a fireplace and small, useful kitchen. Besides your own voices, the only sounds you are likely to hear are the breeze rustling in the trees, the waves lapping the shore, and the occasional horn of a tug or ship as it passes by on a cloudy morning. Fresh-baked delectables are delivered to your door every morning, and eggs, bacon, breads and orange juice are stocked in your refrigerator for your own try at down-home cooking. The Cabin is *THE* place in Port Townsend to spend a truly romantic interlude together.

OLD CONSULATE INN

313 Walker At Washington, Port Townsend 98368
(206) 385-6753
Reasonable to Expensive

Take Highway 20 off of Highway 101 to get to Port Townsend. In town,
Highway 20 then becomes Sims Way. On your left, before you enter the
town, Washington Street branches off and heads up the hill that overlooks
the waterfront. Follow this road up about three blocks to Walker Street.

There are many Victorian homes lining the streets on the hill just
above the downtown section of Port Townsend. Some have been
converted into gracious bed & breakfasts that are cultured and regal,
or, depending on your Victorian viewpoint, opulent and just a little
gaudy. If you are smitten with the idea of surrounding yourselves with
all the pampering nuances of days gone by and intoxicating creature
comforts, then the Old Consulate Inn is exactly right for you.

Upon entering you will be struck by the Inn's affable character —
the music room with its antique organ and grand piano, the fireplace-
warmed study, the reading nook in the front parlor and the wood
tables in the breakfast dining area. Elegant period antiques abound,
but never to excess. The morning meal is a gastronomic fantasy come
true. The Inn has its own blend of designer coffee that it proudly
serves along with five full courses of: fresh fruits, liqueur cakes,
pastries, egg bakes, homemade granolas and an appropriate sherry or
liqueur for finishing the repast with gusto.

At the top of the grand oak staircase, each spacious private room
(eight in all), each with its own bath, is a retreat you need leave
only for breakfast: Sitting alcoves, turret lookouts, canopied king
beds, expansive views of the waterfront and oversized, comfortable
furnishings make the Old Consulate Inn an indulgent overnight
sojourn with yesterday and each other.

◆ **ROMANTIC ALTERNATIVE: James House Bed & Break-**
fast, 1238 Washington Street, Port Townsend 98368, (206)
385-1238 (Reasonable to Expensive), has often been thought of as

one of the finest bed & breakfasts in Port Townsend, and for a while it was. Now in need of some attention to the interior and some variety to the standard continental morning fare, the James House has come down a few notches. Still a handsome building, with lovely period pieces and capacious rooms, it remains a romantic alternative if the Old Consulate Inn is booked.

CHETZEMOLKA PARK

Follow Water Street east through downtown Port Townsend until it dead-ends just before the marina. Go north on Monroe Street for seven short blocks and then east on Blaine for a block to the park.

I told a group of people I was off to explore romantic locations on the Olympic Peninsula. Within moments, one of them slipped me a note that read, "There are parks and then there are parks, but there is only one Chetzemolka," and I agree. This ocean-flanked park is an engrossing combination of the things that make picnicking a treasured outing for two people. Particularly two people who love aesthetically appealing surroundings that enhance the flavors of cheese, fruit and wine. Here you can wander through scattered pinery along a cliff with an eagle's view of Admiralty Inlet and Whidbey Island off on the horizon. The landscape replete with thick grass, a foot bridge over a babbling brook, a few well-spaced picnic tables and swings are what make this traditional, picturesque park a standout. Whether your penchant is for a playful or a peaceful diversion, you will be pleased by Chetzemolka Park.

THE PAVILION

630 Water Street, Port Townsend 98368
(206) 385-4881
Moderate to Expensive

On Water Street in the heart of Port Townsend on the north side of the street.

The Pavilion is a relatively new restaurant in Port Townsend but it looks like it will soon be regarded as one of the most romantic. In keeping with the modest quality of the town, the composure of this location, in a tastefully renovated building, is unobtrusive and refined. The two-tiered, red-brick room is simply adorned with cloth-covered tables. The pace is easy-going but the food will arouse your emotions. Fresh food is a basic to everything served here from the herbs to the fish. The chef keeps the presentations simple and the ingredients interesting, like gorgonzola cheese sauces over linguini or white wine sauce sparked with tarragon and brandy, which keeps the true taste of the food alive and flavorful.

♦ **ROMANTIC OPTION:** The waterfront alternative to the Pavilion is just down the street in a narrow brick building that overlooks the ferry traffic to and from Whidbey Island. It is called **The Lido, 925 Water Street, Port Townsend 98638, (206) 385-7111** (Moderate), and has been a reliable, quaint dining spot in Port Townsend for a while. It is a quiet, cozy corner of the town where the ocean is the accompaniment to every part of your meal.

DEER PARK

Deer Park is southeast of Port Angeles in the Olympic National Park. From Highway 101 turn south at the sign for Deer Park. The park is at the end of this 17-mile drive.

The 17-mile drive to Deer Park is not being recommended without a warning. Countless switchbacks and sharp turns resemble a pretzel more than a road. Plus the road is predominantly unpaved. With conditions like this you need to be guaranteed that at the end there's a payoff to make the ordeal worthwhile. Rest assured there is, and suffer this road's indignities. The reward on a clear day is far greater than you could hope for.

The road meanders up and around exhibiting an enthralling view deep into the heartland of the Olympics. Because of the road conditions you are likely to be quite alone on this infrequently traveled mountain passage. Most everyone else will drive the paved road to Hurricane Ridge, (which has an absolutely astounding view of the Olympics) due south of Port Angeles just off Highway 101. Consequently, the two of you can take in the purple mountain majesty splendor in secretive outdoor privacy.

NOTE: Ask at the ranger station (open in summer only) about the arduous hike up to Blue Mountain. The summit has a view your sore thighs will thank you for, but only after you get to the top.

OLYMPIC HOT SPRINGS

Just southwest of Port Angeles on Highway 101 follow the signs to the Elwha campgrounds. Stay on this road past the ranger station and for another four miles around Lake Mills. There the road will dead-end. Park your car along the side of the road, where you are likely to see a handful of other parked vehicles. The old road ahead, now in remnants, continues for 2.4 miles uphill to the hot springs.

There seems to be some kind of delirious urge in people of this region to soak in an outdoor hot tub, fashioned by nature's thermodynamic best, but to be completely honest, I don't understand why. Even when these bubbling springs of earth-heated water are located in the midst of piercing scenery, the smell of sulphur is piercing enough to make you sick. And then there's the problem, even in remote places, of running into people you wouldn't want to run into in your bathtub, not to mention the thought of sitting on a *who-knows-what's-lurking-on-the-bottom* of the pool you're daring to enter. Well, in spite of all this, my aquatic husband, and my non-aquatic self, ventured up to Olympic Hot Springs on his insistence that I didn't know what I was missing, and that I would be doing a disservice to the book not to go. That clinched it, nothing was going to keep me from simmering in a mud-bottomed, smelly pool of lava-heated water.

The uphill walk was through pretty forest, and because we had started late in the day, we saw a number of drip-drying people heading back who left us with words of encouragement, "Not much farther," "It's great, keep going." As we crossed a log bridge over the effervescent waters of the Elwha River, the aroma of the nearby springs came wafting over us like a lead balloon. The stone-and-log-enclosed pools were tiered on the side of a hill in varying temperature ranges. My husband ran ahead, stripped down to his swimsuit, and enthusiastically dove in.

I was surprised how clean the water looked. It seemed that the water surging up from the earth's center kept a constant fresh flow going by spilling the old water over the rim. The bottom wasn't that muddy, though yes, the odor was omnipresently offensive. And to my surprise my skin did feel silky smooth and we didn't see another person for the entire time we were there. So, do I think it's romantic? Well, my husband does — I guess that's half the battle.

LAKE CRESCENT AND
LAKE CRESCENT LODGE

HC-62, Box 11, Port Angeles 98362-9798
(206) 928-3211
Moderate to Expensive

On the northern edge of the Olympic National Park, accessible just off Highway 101. When you approach Lake Crescent look for the signs indicating the way to the Lodge.

The scenery around Lake Crescent is so riveting it makes you want to spend a day watching the water change colors with the sun's excursion across the sky. A sunny day here may wreak havoc on your senses and emotions. Lake Crescent Lodge rests on the bank of the lake and from your white shingled cabin, heated by a wood stove or a stone fireplace, you can view this glassy stretch of water that curves around forested mountains staggered endlessly in the distance. Inhale deeply to relish the fragrant air that penetrates this epic landscape. The bond you and your loved one create amid all this beauty can elicit dreamy memories with a mere mention of the name Lake Crescent.

If you're just passing through, stop at the Lodge's attractive restaurant and savor a delicious traditional mountain breakfast with robust fresh coffee (a rare find outside of a major city or town), a wholesome lunch or an interesting selection of dinner items from king salmon to Hood Canal oysters in a smooth remoulade.

NOTE: The Roosevelt Fireplace Cottages are definitely the most romantic at the Lodge.

SECOND NOTE: The drive around the lake is a monumental treat. Take the time to see the whole thing and refresh yourself with a swim in summer or take an energetic hike at other times the rest of the year. Be sure to check seasonal availability.

CAPE FLATTERY

Highway 101 intersects with Highway 112 a few miles west of Port Angeles. Take Highway 112 west along the coast to the town of Sekiu. Twenty miles west beyond Sekiu is Neah Bay, and 8.5 miles northwest from there is Cape Flattery.

Sekiu is a small, unassuming fishing town with a handful of motels lining the dock. The town is only 28.5 miles from the northwestern tip of the continental United States, which makes it the gateway to some of the most scintillating scenery anywhere. Drive ahead to Neah Bay just so you can gaze along the Strait of Juan De Fuca, flanked on one side with a menagerie of immutable shore and rugged inlets, and on the other with Vancouver Island's striking mountainous profile. But don't stop here, the best is yet to come.

Drive farther northwest to Cape Flattery, where you can camp or just stop long enough to embrace and behold nightfall. A 30-minute hike down a wooded trail brings you to an astounding corner of the world. Your city temperaments will mellow as you watch the cinematic color change over the rock-strewn beach, with daylight dimming to the fading hues of dusk beyond Tatoush Island.

SHI SHI BEACH

Seven miles southwest of Neah Bay is some semblance of a parking area with signs for the Beach. Right over the embankment next to this parking lot is an expansive, empty beach on Makah Bay. From the parking lot you hike through the three miles of forest and beach trail to Shi Shi.

This eight-mile stretch of untainted beach rivals, in its magnitude and overwhelming presence, any beach along the entire West Coast of the States. There really are no adjectives eloquent enough to describe this penetrating, eternal view of haystack rocks by the hundreds eroded into fascinating statuesque forms; or the jagged cliffs, lush forest colors, white silky sand and tumultuous waves creating an erratic shoreline . . . This needs to be seen to be believed. And because it takes a bit of stamina to get there, you might find yourselves alone, at the edge of the world.

3RD BEACH

*Follow the signs on Highway 101 to La Push, on the northwestern coast
of the Olympic Peninsula. There is only one road heading south of La
Push along the coast. Two miles down this road is a small, barely noticeable
sign indicating 3rd Beach. An unmarked parking area is located at the head
of the trail down to the Beach. A 3/4-mile walk through forest brings you
to the Beach.*

A dear friend, whom I used to jog with, introduced me to 3rd
Beach several summers ago. He is a gentle, sensitive man who loves
G-d's earth like no one I have ever met before. When his city life
becomes too crazy, he often reclaims his sanity in the wilderness,
backpacking, alone. He has a never-failing instinct for survival and
a reverence for nature. I always remember him telling me that 3rd
Beach was one of his favorite places. When I arrived there I
understood why.

You can run barefoot for two miles along the surf that rolls on the
firm sand beneath your strides. There are hidden caves and rock
formations to explore along the way. At low tide, you can climb onto
what at high tide had been islands. Here, pools of trapped sea life
create small aquariums for inquisitive minds to marvel at. As is true
with any angel-sent outing, day's end will come too soon; be sure to
take a seashell or some weather-aged sea stones back with you as a
keepsake of your beautiful time together.

HOH RAIN FOREST

On Highway 101 south of Forks, on the northwest side of the Olympic National Forest, look for signs directing you to the Hoh Visitor Center, which is 19 miles east of the highway. Inquire there about the different hikes available for your skill level.

The entire length of highway from the coast into the Hoh Rain Forest is a kingdom of treasures. The road travels along the evocatively carved river called the Hoh. Where the road ends is the promise of a glorious cathedral-like forest. When you arrive, solemn moss-laden trees of hemlock, some reaching 300 feet in height and 23 feet in circumference, spruce, fir, alder and maple, all extending heavenward, will greet you. On a rare sun-possessed day, misty streams of prismatic light penetrate this thick foliage like sunbeams through stained glass windows.

The Hoh Rain Forest is a thriving example of the potency of moisture when united with nature's beguiling need to produce abundant life. Every inch of ground, including decaying trees, is covered with lichens, ferns and sorrel. As you pass through this forest canopy, there is no holding back the joy and passion you will feel with every step. There is also no holding back the moisture that oozes from the ground with every step. Waterproof shoes will help keep the forest's beauty in perspective and off your socks.

KALALOCH LODGE

HC-80, Box 1100, Forks 98331
(206) 962-2271
Moderate to Expensive

The town of Kalaloch is northwest of Quinault and south of the Hoh River
Valley. The Lodge is on the west side of the road directly off Highway 101.

The Washington Coast is Kalaloch's front yard entertainment.
During low tide, the walk down to the water is a long, sandy hike
accompanied by seagulls drifting overhead. At high tide, the ocean
performs a constant rhapsody that resounds in the air. The main
building, which has a handful of hotel-like accommodations and a
mediocre oceanside restaurant, and the numerous cabins and duplex
units, some with fireplaces, many with views, all very comfortable,
are positioned on a solid rocky dune overlooking a pounding surf,
sovereign sunsets and an ethereal landscape.

In the evening after dinner, light a fire, turn the lights down low
and begin an impetuous night of ghost stories, giggling and cuddling.
Next morning, the mood of the weather will bring either a cool,
penetrating breeze or a warm, soothing sun. For the former, have a
fireside breakfast in your cozy cabin; for the latter, prepare a picnic
brunch to eat on the shore.

LAKE QUINAULT LODGE

P.O. Box 7, South Shore Road, Quinault 98575
(206) 288-2571, 1-(800) 562-6672
Moderate to Expensive

South of Kalaloch on Highway 101, on the east side of the road, you first pass the North Shore Road of Lake Quinault. A few more miles south, turn east on South Shore Road. Proceed two miles to the Lodge.

This isn't the fanciest lodge you will ever stay at, and you may want to call first to be sure a convention group isn't booked at the same time you are. You'll also want to reserve a room in the older section of the lodge where the rooms are quaint but small and avoid the newer rooms which are ultra-tacky but comfortable. Still, what more could someone with tender intentions require than an over-sized, cedar-shingle mansion in rustic decor, showcasing a stone fireplace that overlooks a mountain lake cradled in an evolutionary master-piece, the Olympic Rain Forest? Not enough? Add to that numerous, eerily intriguing hikes to explore after a prolonged breakfast or lunch (be sure to order the standard items from the menu, this restaurant doesn't do well if it has to mix more than three ingredients at a time). And on a clear day, include a lake cruise just before sunset, which will arouse your senses and soothe your tempers. Still something missing? Just nuzzle against that certain someone to quickly forget which way lies civilization and realize that sometimes location and that someone are all you really need.

SCENE-HOPPING RECOMMENDATIONS: Start your trip in **Port Townsend** and stay a night or two at **The Cabin** or **Old Consulate Inn.** Then drive to **Deer Park** and marvel at the compelling view. At day's end settle in at **Lake Crescent Lodge** and enjoy a dinner at the Lodge's restaurant. Another adventure awaits the next morning at **Shi Shi Beach** where you can spend a full day of hiking, playing in the surf and building sand castles. Finish the evening in a cabin at **Kalaloch Lodge,** with your own private dinner that you stir up yourselves.

> "To be a lover is not to make love, but to find a new way to live."
>
> Paul La Cour

continues

BAINBRIDGE ISLAND

VASHON ISLAND

The above is listed alphabetically, the descriptions that follow are arranged by island, from north to south.

THE SAN JUAN ISLANDS

In the San Juan archipelago alone there are over 172 islands. These islands are stunning in their varied, mountainous terrain, force of character and bustling village settings. As you circumnavigate by ferryboat the most popular island grouping, which includes Orcas, San Juan and Lopez, the profound nature of the land as seen from the water will impress you with images of the island-dotted Caribbean — a notable difference being that the San Juans are much more spectacular in their dimension and topography. Of course, you won't see any palm trees here, and since you're about as far north as you can go in the continental United States, the blush in your cheeks will be from the cold and not equatorial heat. But so much the better: cold cheeks give you a snuggling advantage!

Deciding on one ideal place for your pilgrimage won't be an easy task. You can opt for the comfort of the more populated islands, or if you own or have chartered a boat, you can homestead one of the lesser-known islands, setting up camp for a more back-to-basics holiday. Wherever you put down roots in the heart of these waters, you have made the correct choice. The only mistake would be not sharing it side by side with your partner. (Of course, solitary soul-searching is also terrific, but not a great option when affection is the goal.)

DUCK SOUP INN

3090 Roche Harbor Road, San Juan Island 98250
(206) 378-4878
Moderate

Take the ferryboat from Anacortes to Friday Harbor on San Juan Island. The ferry traffic exits onto Spring Street. Turn right onto Second, and follow the signs to Roche Harbor Road. Heading north on Roche Harbor Road, continue for five miles to the restaurant.

On San Juan Island there are two well-established places to dine that pose a dilemma for hungry "lovebirds" everywhere. Both the Duck Soup Inn and Winston's (see next entry) boast gourmet eating opportunities — but that's not the dilemma. The dining circumstances, on the other hand, are a different story. These two spots, though only a few miles apart, are like opposite ends of the world.

If your taste buds and other senses (including your heart) long for an authentic Northwest rustic ambience and savory fresh entrees that change daily, Duck Soup Inn is your answer. The restaurant is a wood-frame country home totally removed from the mainstream of tourist gatherings. The country interior decor and relaxed service create an easy, tasteful atmosphere in contrast to the slightly more elegant feel of Winston's.

NOTE: Check seasonal hour changes.

WINSTON'S

95 Nichols, Friday Harbor, San Juan Island 98250
(206) 378-4073
Moderate

As you exit the ferry dock at Friday Harbor, follow Spring Street and turn right onto Nichols. The restaurant is two blocks west of the ferry dock.

Winston's is a subdued two-story Victorian renovation in the heart of Friday Harbor. It has a *Gatsbyish* feeling about it that is inviting and attractive. The interior is done in soft pastels with flickering candles illuminating the dimly lit room. The menu runs the gamut from standard continental fare to exotic ethnic specialties. In short, this restaurant exemplifies casual island sophistication.

Whether you choose Duck Soup Inn or Winston's, your palatal needs will be beautifully tended to. All you have to do is let your hearts choose the style and atmosphere. Then sit back and let the rest of the affair take care of itself.

LONESOME COVE RESORT

5810-A Lonesome Cove Road, San Juan Island 98250
(206) 378-4477
Moderate to Expensive

From the ferry dock at Friday Harbor, follow the signs to Roche Harbor.
Just before you enter the Harbor, turn right on Rouleau Road. Two miles
east of Roche Harbor turn right at Limestone Point Road and then left on
Lonesome Cove Road.

This is rustic living that is striking in its secluded island comfort. Don't be surprised if you find yourselves with no one else around. The cabins reside on a sandy beach, built 20 feet beyond high tide. Lonesome Cove is enveloped by several acres of dense forest that opens to a clearing of manicured lawns extending down to the water. It will be impossible to ignore the potential for exploring, arm-in-arm, this undisturbed terrain of trees, beach and rocks.

The cabins are assembled like village hideaways and they are all genuinely homespun. Their prime assets are fireplaces and big, old glass windows that overlook Speiden Channel, Speiden Island and, off at the limit of vision, Vancouver Island. By the way, the name of this resort tends to be misleading; with the right someone, lonesomeness is not even vaguely possible.

WESTWINDS BED & BREAKFAST 〰〰〰〰

4909-H Hannah Highlands Road,
Friday Harbor, San Juan Island 98250
(206) 378-5283
Expensive

Call for reservations and directions.

After I describe this perfect island retreat to you, do not be angry
that there is only one suite available. You may be pleased to note
that it is not well-known and therefore you still have a chance at a
reservation. This wood and glass home rests on top of a hill in the
middle of the island. The magnificent view is so vibrant from every
corner of the house's inside that it becomes an integral part of the
interior. Your room is large and tastefully designed so as not to conflict
with the outside. There are french doors that open to a private deck
where you can lull away the morning over an excessive breakfast.
This is truly a desirable island getaway.

ROCHE HARBOR RESORT
RESTAURANT

P.O. Box 1, Roche Harbor, San Juan Island 98250
(206) 378-2155
Moderate to Expensive

From Anacortes, ferry to Friday Harbor. At the ferry dock follow the traffic up Spring Street and turn right at Second Street. At Tucker Avenue turn right again and stay to your left at the fork; this will put you on Roche Harbor Road. You will come to a "T" eight miles down this road, where you turn right, to the village of Roche Harbor. Turn left at the arches to the resort.

Roche Harbor is two miles from Lonesome Cove Resort and is a complete turnabout from the concealment there. This historic harbor and marina is a yachting playground. Every inch of the area that isn't lined with boats is covered with gazebos, rose gardens, sculpted hedges and ivy-laden buildings. Winding brick pathways weave throughout this New Englandesque resort-scape.

Roche Harbor Restaurant is San Juan Island's premier port of call. You will be inclined to dally here for a while on the deck over morning coffee or afternoon tea. When the restaurant is open, the handsome interior, gentle harbor view and fresh food will encourage you to make an entire day of it. This is indeed a reposeful spot from which to watch the comings and goings in the scenic, barrier-island-protected marina.

ROMANTIC WARNING: The main hotel is old and musty, and the newer, expensive rental condos down the road are okay but nothing to write home about. Consider staying at Lonesome Cove or Westwinds and enjoy a meal or two at this location instead.

AMERICAN CAMP

On San Juan Island, from Friday Harbor, follow the ferry traffic on Spring Street to Argyle Road, turning left. This road jogs around and becomes Cattle Point Road, where you turn left again and proceed directly to American Camp.

The heavily forested terrain in the northern section of San Juan Island gives way to the windswept leas carpeted with poppies, wildflowers and waving, waist-high grass at the island's southern extremity, called American Camp. Once you arrive your options are to walk down to the enormous sandy beach and investigate the shoreline and cold Sound waters, or to meander through the spacious meadows that are a mix of sand hills and sea grass. The many opportunities for ducking out of sight make this a perfect camp for lovers. From your personal nook on a cliff, or as you wander along mesmerized by the glorious view of the Olympics, you can watch the sun's procession from morning to dusk as it bathes the hills in a crescendo of parading colors.

MOUNT CONSTITUTION

On Orcas Island, from the ferryboat landing, go north on Horseshoe Highway to the town of Eastsound. Loop around the Bay and head south, following signs to the mountain, which is in the center of Moran State Park.

The road into Moran State Park will lead you to the tallest elevation on the Washington islands, Mount Constitution. Atop its easily attained summit is a stone-masoned lookout tower that takes you well above the trees. From Mount Constitution's peak you see a paragon of island vistas. For 360 degrees the geographical profiles of the Northwest are plainly and stupendously visible. To the east are the majestic Cascades; to the north, Vancouver Island demands your attention; and to the west, looming on the horizon, are the Olympics. Below you are the San Juans and above is the endless Alpine sky.

NOTE: Mount Constitution is a well-visited frontier. For a less-touristed encounter, hike the mountaintop trails and claim a landmark for your own.

ROSARIO ISLAND RESORT
RESTAURANT

Eastsound, Orcas Island 98245
(206) 376-2222
Breakfast and Lunch/Moderate
Dinner/Expensive — Resort/Expensive

From the ferryboat landing go north on Horseshoe Highway to Eastsound,
loop around the water and head south. Rosario Resort is about five miles
down the road.

I would not be the first or the last person to rave about Rosario
Resort's location and views. I also would not be the only person to
warn you about the accommodations that are very expensive and
okay, but far from great, especially considering the price. And I'm
probably not the first to comment on the restaurant, but I can't resist:
Having a corner table, near the floor-to-ceiling windows that expose
a sparkling view of the area, is enough to fill anyone's heart for the
day or night. Yes, the food is American-standard, but with a flavorful
edge that makes it more than ordinary. The service is quite adequate
and if nothing else, it tries hard. All in all, this is a great place for
a morning or afternoon time-out from your day's activities.

TURTLEBACK FARM INN

Route 1, Box 650, Eastsound, Orcas Island 98245
(206) 376-4914
Moderate to Expensive

From the ferry dock follow Horseshoe Highway and turn left on McNallie Road. At Crow Valley Road turn right and watch for the sign indicating the Inn.

This is a delightful place to be on a Northwest morning with the sun just beginning to warm the air and the colors of the countryside coming alive with the glow of daybreak. Turtleback Inn was renovated with country warmth and love in mind. The rooms and private baths range from charming to more charming. The Inn's setting of pastoral peacefulness will make your time here welcomed and remembered. If your hearts and heads are still in doubt, the plentiful breakfasts will convince the rest of you. The likelihood is that you will be wholly thrilled with Turtleback Inn.

SEVENGATES FARM RESTAURANT

Route 1, Box 122E, Eastsound, Orcas Island 98245
(206) 376-2077
Very Reasonable to Moderate

From the ferry dock stay on Horseshoe Highway. Drive past the town of Eastsound for two miles till you come to a stop sign earmarked by a spray-painted water tank in front of you, and turn right. The restaurant will be on your right immediately after you turn.

During one of my romantic missions to Orcas Island I stopped into the Sevengates Farm Restaurant for a quick breakfast. I wasn't expecting anything to knock my socks off: The exterior and interior reflected the late-'60s generation and was much in need of improvement. Nevertheless, the food was surprisingly fresh, generously served and quite tasty. Even the coffee was good and that's always a reliable beginning.

Well, since that morning, the place has undergone a face-lift, particularly the outside deck, which has successfully transformed Sevengates from funky to somewhat contemporary. The menu remains the same mix of hearty breakfast egg dishes and fresh pastry; in the evening pastas and fish fill the menu, with a few Oriental dishes tossed in. Oh, and the setting too is agreeably the same — nestled out in the middle of a golden field, a stone's throw from the ocean, with the powerful shapes of the mountains beyond. As the owner correctly stated, the view is 50 percent of the inside.

THE TOWN OF LANGLEY

Thirty miles north of Seattle, take the Mukilteo ferry to the town of Clinton on Whidbey Island. Five miles north on Highway 525 is Langley.

People with an unromantic disposition may describe Langley as a one-horse town. And they would be right. It just depends on what kind of horse they had in mind. You could say this small, unfettered town, only two blocks in length, is like an independent stallion grazing free, without traditional touristy compromises to break its spirit. Langley is a one-of-a-kind town that still exhibits an undaunted Northwest look and style. There is nothing in the vicinity for miles around to get in your way or spoil the scenery.

Langley resides on the water's edge, and from its meadows and bluffs are amazing views of Mount Baker, the Cascades and the Saratoga Passage. The quality and appeal of this town are in its unaffected style of buildings and stores. On display here is pure Northwestern dedication to flair and detail. As you travel through Whidbey Island, don't let this extraordinary place go by without a visit.

◆ **ROMANTIC OPTIONS:** The accommodations in Langley, hands down, are some of the best places for affection and romance I have seen anywhere. There are almost too many to mention. My absolute favorites are:

Caroline's Country Cottage Bed & Breakfast, 215 6th Street, P.O. Box 459, Langley 98260, (206) 221-8709 (Very Moderate). This is a lovely, country-elegant home just a few blocks from town. The rooms are truly suites where the nights can be filled with fantasy and whimsy. There are also delicious breakfasts and a large hot tub moored in a garden setting.

Eagle's Nest Inn Bed & Breakfast, 3236 E. Saratoga Rd., Langley 98260, (206) 321-5331 (Very Moderate). This newly constructed home sits high on a hill on the outskirts of Langley. The views from the deck and the hot tub are, without exaggeration, spectacular. The house is huge and the rooms spacious. Some have balconies, private entries, and views and all are a great place to call home for a few days of time alone.

The Whidbey Inn Bed & Breakfast, 106 First Street, Langley 98260, (206) 221-7115 (Moderate to Expensive). Reputedly one of Whidbey Island's finest, this inn assuredly ranks with the most interesting. In the heart of Langley, it resides on a bluff with almost every unit featuring scintillating views of simply everything north, south and east. The standard rooms are nice but the three romantic suites are remarkable. The Saratoga Suite, complete with bay windows, marble fireplace and cozy, posh English furnishings is phenomenal. Gourmet breakfasts are delivered to every room for a private, leisurely morning meal.

Lone Lake Cottage & Breakfast, 5206 South Bayview Road, Langley 98260, (206) 321-5325 (Moderate). This eclectic assortment of accommodations five miles outside of town is the most remote and unique place to stay in Langley. Stay in one of the two cottages with fully equipped housekeeping units, and complete with fireplace, deck, VCR and stereo. Or, for a real change of pace, stay on the glass-enclosed houseboat. Each place is a total escape and the setting a sheer joy. Lone Lake doesn't mean alone, it means lovingly together with only the two of you for company.

CLIFF HOUSE

**5440 South Grigware Road, Freeland, Whidbey Island 98249
(206) 321-1566**
Expensive

*Take I-5 north from Seattle to Mukilteo. Take the Mukilteo ferry to
Clinton on Whidbey Island. Follow Highway 525 for 10.6 miles to Bush
Point Road. Turn left and drive 1.5 miles to Grigware Road, where you
turn left again. The road dead-ends; turn right at the brown mailbox and
follow the winding driveway down to Cliff House.*

Bed & breakfasts are usually a preferable change of pace from the
run-of-the-mill hotels and motels that line city streets. The Cliff
House is not only a dramatic change of venue but it alters the entire
concept of what bed & breakfasts are all about. This is a sensuous,
architecturally renowned, Northwest contemporary home, where the
owner turns the keys over to you and you alone and you have solitary
run of the place. (The owners live in an adjacent property.) Except
for the aromas of freshly baked muffins and steeping tea, the two of
you, for all intents and purposes, are hidden away on 13 acres of
total, enviable island exclusivity.

◆ **ROMANTIC SUGGESTION:** Minutes away from the Cliff
House on the west side of the island is the **Bush Point Restaurant,
P.O. Box 1042, Freeland, 98249, (206) 221-2626** (Moderate). It
sits atop a bluff and has a commanding view of the sunset and all
the open waters due west of Whidbey Island. There is dancing and
good food or just a simple nightcap waiting for the two of you any
evening you happen to be looking for an enticing way to while away
the time.

GUEST HOUSE
BED & BREAKFAST COTTAGES ❤❤❤❤

835 East Christenson Road, Greenbank, Whidbey Island 98253
(206) 678-3115
Moderate to Expensive

From Seattle, take I-5 north to the Mukilteo ferry dock and take the ferry to Clinton. Once on the island, follow Highway 525 16 miles to Christenson Road. Visible from the highway on the west side of the road is the yellow farmhouse where the office is located.

This is another one of those places I almost passed up. The unassuming yellow house that is only a few feet from the road looked relatively uninviting and noisy. I have learned from this experience to never pass up anything based solely on its outer appearance, because what is inside may be more precious and august and far-reaching than I could have dreamed possible. The Guest House is just such a place. Yes, the road-frontage exterior was drab, but the idyllic, cozy log cabins and wondrous log home set amongst 25 acres of meadow and forest were some of the most nostalgic kissing places I've yet seen.

These uniquely authentic log homes are something out of a storybook — brimming with petite kitchens, VCRs, fireplaces, oak furniture, stained glass windows, knotty pine walls, decks and all the charm you could ever want. Breakfast is stocked in your rooms with all the ingredients fresh and abundant. As if that weren't enough, there are a hot tub and swimming pool on the property as well.

Three of these cottages are small, intimate quarters; the fourth is a log mansion without comparison anywhere in the Northwest. This capacious home is the ultimate experience in togetherness. The huge stone fireplace, large soaking tub, antique wonders everywhere, floor-to-ceiling windows and full gourmet kitchen are absolutely fabulous.

ROMANTIC OUTING: One mile north of the Guest House is **Whidbey's Greenbank Farm, Ranch 5, Loganberry Farm, Greenbank 98253 (206) 678-7700.** This is a vineyard par excellence with a delightful tasting room and idyllic picnic grounds. If you can pull yourself away from your log cabin for a few hours, a sweet afternoon is there for the sipping.

COLONEL CROCKETT FARM INN 💋💋💋💋

1012 South Fort Casey Road,
Coupeville, Whidbey Island 98239
(206) 678-3711
Reasonable to Moderate

From Seattle take I-5 north to Mukilteo and ferry to Clinton. Follow Highway 525 for 23 miles. Turn left onto Highway 20. After 1.4 miles turn right onto Wanamaker Road and drive 1.7 miles. Turn left onto South Fort Casey Road for two miles. Watch carefully for the sign in front and then turn left into the Farm's driveway.

As you pull into the driveway ignore the dilapidated red barn that has, to say the least, seen better days. It is nothing more than an eyesore and will melt away as you enter this consummate, elegant country home, renovated specifically to be the essence of gracious living. The colors, appointments, hand-crafted wood paneling, private baths and loving personal touches combine to assure a sublime time away from everything except each other.

PLEASANT BEACH GRILL
AND OYSTER BAR

4738 Lynnwood Center Road, Bainbridge Island 98110
(206) 842-4347
Expensive

*From the Winslow ferry dock, go to the first light and turn left. Head
through the town of Winslow and turn right on Madison Street. At the
next stoplight turn left on Wyatt. Follow this road as it curves around,
then follow the signs to Lynnwood. Watch for the sign indicating the
restaurant.*

This is an English tudor-style restaurant, skillfully renovated from
what was once an old, secluded mansion. Yet, the atmosphere and
food are a Northwest experience from start to finish. You are served
in what was formerly the estate's living room. Beautifully arranged
about this room are linen-draped tables accented with china and
crystal. As formal as this description may sound, the mood and pace
are relaxed and comfortable; nothing stuffy is to be found here.
Attentive hospitality and imaginative, fresh food are the calling card
of this establishment. Their half dozen or so exotic oyster concoctions
alone are worth a trip.

After dinner you can step down into the restaurant's fireside lounge
and sink into one of the leather sofas that surround the stone hearth.
Snuggling close together you can relax as the crackling fire casts its
light on the mahogany-paneled room. For an extra treat, when you're
both toasty warm, drive down to the bay and observe the traffic of
ferryboats and a myriad of other vessels passing through the channel.

◆ **ROMANTIC SUGGESTION:** If an overnight island visit is
your desire, you could not escape to a better place than the **Bombay
House Bed & Breakfast, 8490 N.E. Beck Road, Bainbridge Island,
98110, (206) 842-3926** (Moderate). This stately country mansion
resides high on a hill a mile or so from the shore. The rooms are
wonderful, the breakfasts scrumptious and the privacy unsurpassed.

SOUND FOOD
AND POINT DEFIANCE LOOKOUT

Rt. 2, Box 298, Vashon Island 98070
(206) 463-3565
Inexpensive to Moderate

Eight miles straight down the main road of the island from the Vashon ferry dock on the east side of the street at the intersection of 240th and Highway 99.

To start a sunny summer evening off right, take the 6 pm ferry from West Seattle at the Fauntleroy ferry dock across to Vashon Island. (This is only a 15-minute trip, so hurry to the bow of the boat and stand watch on the deck to fully enjoy the crossing.) The ferry will let you off on the main road which runs through the center of the island. Almost to the other end of the island is your standing invitation to Sound Food, a very special, love-filled, health-aware gourmet restaurant. You'll find the country atmosphere, hospitality and freshly prepared food a genuine island-styled change of pace.

After you've taken a leisurely two hours to relish the various subtleties of your meal and indulge in a second helping of fresh-baked bread, a glimpse out the window should reveal the impending sunset. This is the perfect time to drive to the **Point Defiance Lookout.**

Continue along the road that brought you to the restaurant until it ends at the water on the south side of the island. Turn right at the dead end and continue up the hill for about two miles. At the top, keep an eye on the west side of the road for the turnoff. The view from up here, across the Sound, is devastatingly beautiful. What better way to watch a sunset than next to a significant someone, with both of you understanding what a full, contented feeling truly is?

> *"Love doesn't make the world go round*
> *— it's what makes the ride worthwhile."*
> Franklin P. Jones

T H E   C A S C A D E S

The above listings are arranged alphabetically within regions. The following descriptions are in the same regional north to south grouping but the places follow driving routes.

THE CASCADES

The Washington Cascades form one spectacular mountain range.
To the north, Mount Baker's glacial peak looms as a steadfast guardian
near the Canadian-US border. Then traveling south for 200 miles
are the mesmerizing scenery and country landscape of the national
forests, parks and wilderness areas, which include the monolithic
giants: Mount Rainier, Mount St. Helens and Mount Adams. This
chain of mountains patterned with timber, rocky peaks, snow-covered
cliffs, countless plummeting waterfalls and spirited rivers culminates
on the Washington side with the ineffable passage of the Columbia
River Gorge.

The Cascades are a range of radically different climates and colors.
In contrast to the wet, vivid greenery on the west side of the Cascades,
the east side of the mountains is authentic Marlboro country —
draped in hues of gold, bathed in sunshine and accompanied by four
distinct seasons. The northern portion of the range is replete with
Alpine peaks, rolling green hills and acres of traversible wilderness.
The southern portion is a long series of hills and valleys that
intermittently rise up in the form of dominating volcanic peaks . . .
Almost all of this expanse of forest and mountains is beautiful and
almost all of it is overflowing with Northwest activity and tranquility.

Be forewarned that the roads through this massive territory often
lead to visual bliss. The most popular and accessible route for your
eyes is the Cascade Loop, which is a series of connecting highways
through the northern section of the mountains. The Loop's route is
as follows: Starting just south of Everett, take Highway 2 east across
Stevens Pass to the town of Leavenworth on the east side of the
mountains. Watch for the signs directing you to Wenatchee on the
far eastern side of the mountains. Just before Wenatchee take
Highway 97 north past Chelan about 20 miles where you get on
Highway 153 and continue north toward Twisp. Then you take
Highway 20 toward Mazama and begin crossing back west across the
Cascades, eventually to Interstate 5. Technically the Loop continues
out to La Conner and down through Whidbey Island, ending with

a ferryboat ride back to Mukilteo, just south of Everett.

Besides the Loop, there are other, more private, creative options to consider. Contact the National Park Service at 800 State Street, Sedro Woolley, Washington 98284, and have them send you detailed maps of the area. There is a plethora of graveled dirt roads off the main highways that lead you away from the usual to the paths less taken. These are treks of the heart for pleasure and adventure.

♦ **ROMANTIC PRELUDE:** From Seattle, if you are heading out to the Cascades on I-90 and you want to take a moment to get a remarkable overview of what you will be traveling through, consider stopping at **Snoqualmie Winery, 1000 Winery Road, Snoqualmie, (206) 888-4000** (watch for the signs next to the Snoqualmie Falls exit). The view of the mountains from the tasting room is unbelievable, and the wine is a premium accompaniment to the surroundings.

♦ **ROMANTIC ENDING:** On Highway 20, as you finish the last stretch (or the beginning, depending on which direction you started from) of your journey along the Cascade Loop, the **Diablo Dam Overpass** and **Ross Lake** will take your breath away. The vistas along this stretch of road are all a must for some intense staring and humbling sights.

NOTE: After an exhilarating discussion of river rafting in the Cascades, the next several entries take you around a portion of the Loop, starting from Leavenworth in the southeast section and driving up to Mazama on the northeastern side. The entries then jump south to Mount Rainier, finishing at the Washington side of the Columbia River Gorge.

NORTHERN WILDERNESS RIVER RIDERS

13052 164th Avenue N.E., Redmond 98052
(206) 448-RAFT
Expensive

For any of the rivers you may be interested in traveling, call for information and directions for rendezvousing with your guide.

The rivers that make their way through the Cascades provide superlative drama for those daring couples who want a thoroughly titillating form of transportation. Once you've made the decision about which river you want to negotiate, the rest is, if you will, all downhill.

As you follow the tendril-like course the water has etched through the land, each coiling turn exposes a sudden change in the perspective and dynamics of the landscape. One turn may reveal grassy woods following the quiet flow of peaceful water; another magically manifests a rocky, snowcapped tableau, penetrated by a bursting mass of energy called white water . . . And that's just from the road. Once you're in the raft, the roller-coaster sensations accentuate the thrill of just being there.

Conjure in your mind the pure excitement of being amid these constant scenic transformations. Now watch in awe as the rush of propelled movement builds with the increasing potential danger followed by the spray of the crashing water. The sensation of cold water against your skin as you wildly paddle over and through a whirlpool makes your heart pound and your senses spin. Your laughter mingles with the other voices around you, but you are particularly in tune with the sounds of glee from the special person who joined you on this river-rafting expedition.

NOTE: The Skykomish, Klickitat and Methow rivers are among the most incredible rafting trips you'll find. They are both visually exciting and relentlessly tumultuous. There are several river-rafting companies in the Northwest that can professionally guide you down any of the rivers you may want to try. Northern Wilderness is a good, safe company that will provide you with solid information as well as one of their clever brochures.

$300.00
50.00   *148 - 158 mountain*

MOUNTAIN HOME LODGE   ◆◆◆◆

P.O. Box 687, Leavenworth 98826   *148*
(509) 548-7077
Off-Season/Very Reasonable — On-Season/Expensive

Head north from Seattle on Interstate 5, and just south of Everett, take Highway 2 to Leavenworth. East of town, immediately past the bridge over the Wenatchee River, turn right on Duncan Road. Duncan Road will connect with Mountain Home Road, which will take you directly to the lodge. In winter the prearranged pickup area is just west of Duncan Road; call for specific directions to the rendezvous point.

If seclusion is something you dream about and being take care of is what you crave, you can come to Mountain Home Lodge and find out what a perfect balance of the two is like. The substantial wood lodge is cradled atop a private mountain meadow and can graciously tend to all of your dining, athletic and snuggling needs. Your entire stay here will be a little bit of everything but mostly a truly fulfilling time away for both of you.

The only way to reach this location during the winter is by a prearranged snowcat pickup that will rendezvous with you just outside of Leavenworth on Highway 2. From there it is a half-hour trip up the mountainside to the isolated accommodations of the lodge. The slow trip up overlooks the quiet river valley twinkling with lights from the village shops and streets of Leavenworth. Be prepared for a quiet ascent punctuated only by the sounds of crunching snow and your "oohs" and "aahs" of amazement.

When you arrive during winter, the mountain and meadow will

be completely swept over with snow. The steam from the hot tub will drift lazily into the air and disappear. Your room will be unassuming though very comfortable with a view of the snow-covered landscape. The fireplace in the shared living area is next to the small dining room that will serve you three mountain-fresh, country-style meals every day. Wall-to-wall windows allow you to watch the winter weather in its full white glory as you soak up the warmth and hospitality of the interior. Cross-country skiing, snowmobiling and sledding are all at your doorstep. *$40.00 per person*

During the summer months Mountain Home Lodge is easily accessible and can still be just as private and exciting. Without the snow's enchanting limitations, horseback riding, restauranting and hiking are nearby.

NOTE: During the summer the meals are not included in the price of the accommodation so the meals are available to those not staying at the lodge. Breakfast/Moderate — Lunch/Inexpensive — Dinner/Moderate.

ROMANTIC WARNING: There are some who do not think the town of Leavenworth is romantic. I was one of them until I took a closer look. My hesitation was due to the town's Bavarian theme. The Germanic, ski-lodge influence is robust in a beerfest, crowds-galore frame of reference, and it doesn't leave much room for tender snuggling or quiet moments. Still, Leavenworth has something for everyone and you'll find some romantic alternatives that enable the softer side of the town to be yours — like cross-country skiing, hiking, white-water rafting, daydreaming, quiet restaurants, picnics and more.

Haus Lorelei Bed & Breakfast◈◈◈◈

347 Division Street, Leavenworth 98826
(509) 548-5726
Very Reasonable

From Highway 2, as you enter the town of Leavenworth from the west, turn south onto Ninth Street. Go two blocks and turn west onto Commercial and then south again onto Division. Division dead-ends at Haus Lorelei.

The best of both worlds is available at Haus Lorelei. It is just on the border of Leavenworth's town center, yet there will be no evidence of that lively world only moments away. From the moment you enter this European country mansion you will realize that now relaxation is at hand and the stress of the world is somewhere else. This bed & breakfast offers a winter or summer sojourn made up of everything you wanted from time spent together.

The breakfast area and sitting area are partitioned by a massive stone fireplace. There is a huge screened porch that overlooks the expansive lawn and edge of the Wenatchee River below. The sound of rushing white-water can soothe the most stressed city nerves. The bedrooms are huge and comfortable and decorated with magnificent wood antiques imported from Germany. In the morning, as you take time over a breakfast of crepes and fresh fruit, your easygoing hostess can help you plan a rewarding day.

NOTE: All the rooms are wonderful, but the River's Edge room on the second floor is ideal.

◆ **ROMANTIC OPTION: The Terrace Bistro, 200 Eighth Street, Leavenworth 98826** (Lunch/Reasonable — Dinner/Moderate to Expensive) is considered by the townspeople to be the best restaurant for miles around. The upstairs location and rooftop dining area are the scene of a Bavarian-styled hearty time above the crowds.

SILVER BAY INN

Box 43, Stehekin 98852
(509) 682-2212
Inexpensive to Reasonable

Take Highway 2 heading east past Leavenworth, toward Wenatchee. Follow the signs for Highway 97 north. This will take you to the town of Chelan, where you can catch the boat to Stehekin. For information on scheduled departures call (509) 682-2022 or (800)-4CHELAN. Hikers will want to check with the National Park Service for the backpacking route to Stehekin.

What makes this bed & breakfast so decidedly special isn't its solar window construction or cozy, windowed breakfast nook. Neither are the wondrous views from the deck and rooms or the tempting espresso breakfasts the main attraction. Rather it is the extreme isolation of the location that makes this spot a Northwest must for those who want to get away from it all in the truest sense of the word "away."

The town of Stehekin is geographically unique. It is accessible only by ferryboat (no cars) from Chelan, or over the mountains via high-country trails. Lake Chelan is renowned for its glorious, dramatic scenery. The towering mountains that line this 55-mile lake are breathtaking against the cool blue of the glacier-fed waters. The trip and overnight stay are a prerequisite for those who want the pampering of a B&B and the quiet of backpacking country.

NOTE: The exquisite ferry crossing is approximately four hours. There is only one round-trip crossing a day. Stehekin tends to be a bit crowded in the afternoon with the ferry passengers. But because most of the ferry traffic stays only for the day, once the boat leaves again, in the early evening, only the rugged remain and the town is serenely peaceful once more.

Sun Mountain Lodge
and Restaurant

P.O. Box 1000, Winthrop 98862
(509) 996-2211
Off-Season/Reasonable — High-Season/Expensive

Follow Highway 97 north toward Pateros. At Pateros turn northwest onto
Highway 153 and follow the Methow River toward Twisp. Take Highway
20 through Twisp on to Winthrop. From there follow the signs to the Lodge.

The drive up to Sun Mountain Lodge is alone well worth the trip.
The winding road allows for a sweeping view of the rugged, sculpted
mountains and golden valley below. Since you've taken the drive,
you may as well stop for a while at the restaurant and allow your eyes
to feast on the surroundings that are food for the soul. They confirm
that this place has one of the best view-bars in the region. The deck
that wraps around the outside will bring you face to face with the
majesty of the area. Hold hands tightly, this one is truly amazing.

NOTE: The overnight accommodations are on the tacky side, but
some are more than reasonable in price and are worth considering if
the idea of leaving this incredible location becomes too much to bear.
Also, during the winter the cross-country skiing here is fabulous.

◆ **ROMANTIC OPTION:** There are horse-riding stables a
stone's throw from the lodge. For a more Ponderosa-like excursion
through this terrain, a jaunt on horseback is a fun side-attraction.

THE MAZAMA COUNTRY INN

P.O. Box 223, Mazama 98823
(509) 996-2681
Very Inexpensive to Very Reasonable

Fourteen miles north of Winthrop on Highway 20 watch for the signs to the Inn.

The Mazama Inn is in the middle of nowhere and that is one of its most attractive points. It is set in the heart of the forest at the foot of a mountainside. The bedrooms are simple, clean and unassuming, which would be a drawback if it weren't for their sensational views and the Inn's amenities available both winter and summer. Everything is here for you — horseback riding, helicopter skiing, cross-country skiing, mountain bicycling, wind surfing, sleigh riding, and a hot tub and sauna.

The restaurant serves three wonderful meals, to suit each season, with breakfast being a huge feast and dinner offering a creative selection of meats, fresh fish and pasta. The interior is soothing and calming. The outdoors grace the windows with gently swaying boughs and the floor to ceiling stone fireplace keeps the room toasty warm. The Mazama Country Inn is an easy, casual setting for play and sharing quiet, treasured moments.

NOTE: During the winter, the meals are included in one reasonably priced, excellent package.

MOUNT RAINIER NATIONAL PARK

Many roads lead to Mount Rainier: From Enumclaw on the north and Yakima on the east you take Highway 410 into the park. Highway 12 from both the east and west at the southern end of Mount Rainier intersects with Highway 123, which will take you into the park. On the southwest side of the park Highway 7 intersects with Highway 706 at the town of Elbe. Highway 706 goes right into the park and takes you straight to Paradise, literally and figuratively.

The poetic words one might address to this soaring, eternal peak are better left to the laureates. For the purposes of this book and kissing, it is sufficient to say that almost every inch of this mountain is quintessentially romantic and outrageously exquisite. From its volcanic heart to its eternally snow-covered peaks, Mount Rainier is guaranteed to provide superlative panoramic views, memorable hikes and crystal clear lakes . . . If it's Northwest drama and passion you yearn for, name it and this volcano has it.

NOTE: Mount Rainier is only one of several dormant volcanos around these parts. Less traveled than Mount Rainier are Mount Baker, just south of the Canadian border, and Mount Adams, just north of the Oregon border. All three of these mountainlands hold out good prospects for unrestrained messing around.

SECOND NOTE: Several park roads, including some of the main routes onto the mountain, are closed during the winter, so always check seasonal availability. For area information call (206) 569-2211.

CHINOOK PASS

On the east side of Mount Rainier, Highway 410 heading from the Mount Baker-Snoqualmie National Forest goes through Chinook Pass just before it enters Mount Rainier National Park.

On a fall afternoon, Chinook Pass becomes almost too beautiful. You'll be so excited about the scenery you might finish touring and forget to kiss. There is an aura about this section of mountain that floods the senses with a charismatic power. Take a moment to create in your mind the image of golden light bathing hills and lakes. Notice the vivid leaf-shades of red and amber that brocade the trees and meadows. Feel the fall air tickling your skin at the same time solar heat tempers that chill . . . Sigh, this is a visual gift to share together.

NOTE: The drive through the pass is loaded with vista turnoffs, hikes with dizzying switchbacks and leas where you can explore side by side. The only caution is to travel prepared. Comfortable hiking shoes, munchies (lots of munchies), water bottle, tissues and a day-pack will make the Pass a more passable experience.

SUNRISE

From the north or east take Highway 410 into Mount Rainier National Park and follow the park map to Sunrise.

If you've always wondered what it must be like at the top of the world, come to Sunrise and fulfill your fantasy, for this is in fact as close to the top of the world as you can drive to in the continental United States, and you can almost drive there. When you arrive, there are so many beautiful trails (some relatively easy) to pick from that choosing might be harder than you'd like. Your day hike can be a level, leisurely stroll or a strenuous trek on a mountain path, far away from everyone and everything, except each other. You will never hear such tranquil silence as here at Sunrise.

EMERALD RIDGE

This area of Mount Rainier is on the west face of the mountain near the Highway 706 entrance to the park. One mile after you enter the park there will be a left turn that takes you on an unpaved road along Emerald Ridge. This road is open only during the summer.

The entire west side of Mount Rainier is a challenge made for daring companions who own a four-wheel drive jeep or truck. The road is more the remnant of a logging path so it is not often driven on. The trails off of this road are hiked even less. Finding your own special spot will be hard on your car and you, but worth every bounce and the steep ascent.

MIO AMORE PENSIONE

P.O. Box 208, Trout Lake 98650
(509) 395-2264
Very Moderate to Moderate

From Highway 14 on the north side of the Columbia River Gorge, near White Salmon, head north on Highway 141 to Trout Lake. As you enter the town, watch for the signs to Mio Amore.

For some reason Mount Adams isn't lauded as much as the other sights in the Cascades. Yet, this inactive volcano is in a unique position at the south end of the range, sitting astride the green forests of the western side and rain shadow of the eastern half. Wine country adds distinction, surrounding the base of the mountain, and the recreational activities here are as abundant as you could want.

Mio Amore Pensione rests at the foot of Mount Adams, whose snowcapped peaks and rolling hills tower over the back yard. This Victorian home has been renovated into a wonderful bed & breakfast with elegant rooms and tender touches all about. Yet the highlight of your stay will be the three gourmet meals served by the hosts every day. Of course, breakfast is complimentary, and it is graciously served. Lunch is a selection of rich pastas and dinner is an assortment of delicious Italian-styled entrees of veal, chicken, rabbit and fish. This is a relaxing, pampered way to take care of yourselves in Northwest style and seclusion.

NOTE: Reservations for lunch and dinner are accepted even if you are not staying overnight at the Pensione.

◆ **A ROMANTIC MUST:** On your way either to or from Mount Adams, be certain to stop at the **Charles Hooper Family Winery, Spring Creek Road, Husum 98623, (509) 493-2324.** (Call first to check seasonal hours.) A picnic or stroll through the vineyards treats you to one of the most exquisite views you'll behold anywhere. Take the time for this one; your eyes, palates and hearts will be forever grateful.

INN OF THE WHITE SALMON

172 Jewett, White Salmon 98672
(509) 493-2335
Moderate

From Highway 14, follow Highway 141 a short distance to the town of White Salmon. The Inn is at the north end of town on the right hand side of the road.

For romantic purposes, a bed & breakfast needs to be more than just a place that serves a good breakfast. I have never even considered recommending a place simply for that one feature — until now, that is. The Inn of the White Salmon is located on a noisy street in a less-than-attractive part of town. The rooms are old, dark and musty, with no views and no redeeming features. But all of that melts into oblivion when you wake up to the breakfast feast served faithfully every morning in the quaint Inn dining room.

Actually a feast doesn't quite adequately describe the occasion; perhaps a gourmet, sweet-tooth orgy is more like it. The buffet table is likely to sport seven different egg dishes ranging from casseroles to quiches, an arrangement of a dozen or so fresh-baked French pastries and another dozen or so cakes and pies. For the price of a night's stay on your way to Mount Adams or down to the Gorge, this is a banquet both of you will relish long past dinnertime — and for days to come.

Is It Better To Kiss In A Bed & Breakfast Than A Hotel?

Depending on whom you're talking to, the subject of bed & breakfasts conjures up either images of enticing comforts or fears of Ma & Pa Kettle proprietors with homes to match. Each bed & breakfast can have its own special brand of cordiality and sensual touches that are so essential to this type of lodging. And given the right touches, there is nothing quite as affection-producing as staying in a home that diligently tends to matters of the heart.

The problems you may run into with B&Bs are entailed by the varying approaches to homeyness that exist out there. Beds that sink in the middle, furniture that is beyond Victorian, musty maroon carpeting, walls like paper, running into someone you don't know en route to the bathroom or, worse, finding it occupied when you're in need — such are a few of the worst-case scenarios I can think of. In comparison to some hotels, though, even that is preferable.

So, is it better to kiss in a bed & breakfast? Of course, all the bed & breakfasts (and the hotels for that matter) included in this book are superlative places to stay and all the above concerns were addressed before any establishment was even considered for inclusion. But for those of you trying to choose between the types listed in this book, keep in mind that service in hotels is much less personal than in B&Bs. On the other hand, if staying in someone else's home or a small inn is a problem for you, regardless of the circumstances, you won't be able to relax no matter how nice any of the details inside the B&B happen to be.

S E A T T L E

The above list is alphabetical, but the descriptions that follow are arranged loosely around the downtown area heading north.

IL TERRAZZO CARMINE

411 First Avenue South, Seattle 98104
(206) 467-7797
Moderate

In Seattle's Pioneer Square on First Avenue between Jackson and King Streets.

Il Terrazzo Carmine is a poetic city nightspot, right in the middle of what is not the prettiest part of Pioneer Square. Through a brick archway corridor, earmarked by a sign for the New Empty Space Theatre, is a ceramic, aqua-blue-tiled fountain of ponds cascading one into the other. Strategically placed backlighting reflects off the water and makes the patio shimmer and gleam in the night air. This is the restaurant's back yard, where tables are set during the summer. Inside there is even more evidence of romantic detail in the pretty dining room, replete with comfortable rattan chairs, crystal, and floral-patterned china, all arranged to suit close encounters. Rest assured that the food is also an essential part of the atmosphere. The kitchen consistently prepares a combination of traditional and daring Italian dishes, with one of the most exceptional antipasto presentations I've seen and tasted anywhere. After a leisurely evening tour through Pioneer Square, or before the curtain goes up or after the final bow, your evening can easily be centered around the al dente food and glowing ambience of Il Terrazzo Carmine.

WATERFALL GARDEN

Just north of the Kingdome at the intersection of Washington and Main streets on the northwest corner.

Why this lush urban garden exists is anyone's guess, but it does and it is a unique city hideaway. This cloistered oasis is enclosed by stone walls and a gate, yet there is still a pervasive tropical, if not jungle-like, feeling. The large rushing waterfall tumbling over boulders at the back of the garden helps drown out any evidence that a city is somewhere nearby. You can use this place for a rendezvous with someone special before a football game or waterfront dinner, or make it an afternoon picnic spot. The likelihood is you will be fairly alone while you are here.

NOTE: This park closes around 9 p.m.

THE MIRABEAU RESTAURANT

1001 Fourth Avenue, Seattle 98154
(206) 624-4550
Expensive

In downtown Seattle on the 46th floor of the 1001 Fourth Avenue Plaza Building, at the intersection of Fourth Avenue and Madison Street.

Most of the dinner crowd in Seattle, particularly those who have been dining out in the area for some time, will be surprised to see The Mirabeau listed as a best kissing place. It is a vintage restaurant, and though it has always been known for its reliable kitchen, it has also been known for being a bit stuffy. But no more; today a new, softer pastel interior erases all of that stuffiness and the glorious view fills the room with evocative softness, creating one of Seattle's most beautiful places for a pleasurable meal or dessert. At the 46th-floor height, you're almost soaring over the Olympics, Sound and broad cityscape. Roseate-orange sunset colors fill the western sky and set the mountains in intricate relief. As the sunset fades, a dance of lights from the darkening buildings below colorfully enlivens the city night. This setting combined with perfectly cooked salmon, piquant sauces and the one you love is absolutely perfect for romance.

THE FOUR SEASONS OLYMPIC HOTEL

411 University Street, Seattle 98101
(206) 621-1700; 1(800) 223-8772
Expensive to Very Very Expensive

Between Fourth and Fifth avenues on University Street, across from Rainier Square.

This is one outrageously sexy, ultra-posh downtown Seattle hotel. There are over 400 rooms in the opulently renovated landmark building, which is located near everything the city has to offer. The rooms are done in an amiable layout, some having separate sitting rooms; but they are, in the long run, just nice hotel rooms. From the heart's point of view, the suites are not what make this a place to spend a euphoric, swept-away weekend together. Rather the hotel, plainly stated, has the most sensual restaurants, health club and lobby area I've seen anywhere in the Northwest. Once you arrive you won't have a reason to go anywhere else to get your romantic needs met. Starting with the complimentary health club: included are a lap pool, a 20-person Jacuzzi (which seems hardly to be used), a modest workout room and an outdoor lounge, where poolside service mellows an arduous morning's workout into pampered quiet with a cup of fresh coffee and an outstanding eggs Florentine.

For every other meal, **The Garden Court Room** is a radiant composite of tea room, lounge/bistro and weekend ballroom. It is an immense hall, arrayed with a fusion of trees, marble floors, 40-foot-tall luminous windows, a petite waterfall cascading into a marble pond, and well-spaced groupings of settees, cushioned chairs and glass coffee tables. This prodigious dining room changes appearance as the day progresses: morning espresso, midday savory lunch, late afternoon authentic tea service, evening cocktails and late-evening, big-band dancing every Friday and Saturday night.

The Georgian Court is the very grand, very civilized, very distinguished dining room of the hotel, overflowing with crystal chandeliers and monolithic floral arrangements, and diffusely lit. Service includes breakfast, lunch and a five-star dinner, all in a high-brow style you could easily grow accustomed to. The cuisine, particularly Sunday brunch, is inspired, luscious continental dishes, with an emphasis on presentation and kid-glove service . . . When you talk about a romantic package in Seattle, the Four Seasons Olympic is definitely the first choice for a night or two, or three . . .

NOTE: Ask the hotel about its romantic weekend, special-priced packages.

♦ **ROMANTIC OPTION:** To many, the most romantic setting in Seattle includes the Pike Place Market, the waterfront and Elliott Bay with the Olympics serving as backdrop to the whole grouping. For your first visit to Seattle you may want to stay at the center of this city scene and can do so in style at the **Inn at the Market, 86 Pine Street, Seattle 98101, (206) 443-3600, 1(800) 446-4484** (Moderate to Very Expensive). The rooms are fairly ordinary and sparse, with a few nice touches like large armoires and good service tossed in to produce an inn-like feeling. But the location's the thing; for those who want proximity to some of Seattle's landmarks, there's no other place like this one.

MAXIMILIEN-IN-THE-MARKET

85 Pike Street, Seattle 98101
(206) 682-7270
Reasonable to Moderate

In the Pike Place Market on the south end of the arcade facing the water.
Look for the entrance in the area of shops to the left of the clock.

I am always searching for the quintessential romantic breakfast.
The kind of place where mornings succumb to the heart's longing
and the time passes slowly with nothing to do but sip another latte
and find solace in prolonging sunrise for longer than usual. At
Maximilien's, this relaxed attitude is felt at all meals, but especially
breakfast. This modest restaurant, with a small array of wood tables,
walls covered with antique mirrors and a mesmerizing view of the
Sound and Olympics, serves a very French and very delectable
morning meal. Souffles, eggs Benedict, shirred eggs and fresh pastries
are the daily offerings, and Sunday brunch adds a few standard lunch
selections. Sleeping in will never be the same after spending a morning
here.

NOTE: Maximilien's also serves an excellent French dinner that
is reasonably priced and features the Olympics changing color in
harmony with the setting sun.

CAFE DILETTANTE

1600 Post Alley, Seattle 98101
(206) 728-9144, or
416 Broadway, Seattle 98112
(206) 329-6463
Both are Inexpensive

The 1600 Post Alley Cafe is in the Pike Place Market on Pine Street. The 416 Broadway Street location is on Broadway in between Harrison and Republican Streets.

Alright, I admit it, I'm a chocolate lover and even if this place weren't quaint, in an unruffled, sweet, rustic environment, I would still be a fan of the Dilettante. Their chocolates are tastes of fantasy, and outrageous examples of how sugar can be used to torment the palate to excess. Sorry, I'm getting carried away; back to the subject of romance: There are two Dilettante cafes in Seattle, the one on Capitol Hill with its charming wood tables and dimly lit chocolatey-brown interior, and the one in the Market with its marble table tops arced around a glass showcase of creamy morsels. The Capitol Hill location's interior is actually the more romantic in design, but crowds prevent that mood from prevailing. This is frequently regrettable in the evening, when sharing a torte covered in ephemere sauce is the only way to say goodnight, except for a kiss, that is. The cafe in the market is, for some unknown reason, never full and as a result is always nectareously romantic.

THE SORRENTO HOTEL

900 Madison Street, Seattle 98104
(206) 622-6400
Very Expensive

At Madison and Terry streets, about six blocks east of downtown Seattle.

Generally, you can assume that downtown hotels are of two types. One type is slick and corporate, designed to efficiently handle large groups of people or to encourage business types to take care of business. The other model is the more modest establishment with the basic conveniences of bar, restaurant and gift shop that exists solely to facilitate sleep and quick departure in the morning. But every now and then there is an exception to the rule — a smaller, elegant renovation where the mood is intimate and tranquil, and the attention very personal. The Sorrento is such a hotel.

The Fireside Room next to the lobby is a handsome, albeit formal, assortment of settees, sofas and chairs wrapping around an imposing stone and hand-painted-tile fireplace. It is wonderfully inviting for an early evening conversation or an after-dinner aperitif. The restaurant is called **The Hunt Club Room.** It is a seductively lit, bordering on dark, dining room, Honduran-mahogany paneling alternating with brick walls throughout. The service is attentive almost to a fault, the food creative and carefully prepared. Your every need will be obligingly met, including privacy — even the waiters will have trouble seeing you as the lighting is below their eye level. Obviously, it's an understatement to call this restaurant a cozy, gourmet dining experience. Between the lobby bar and The Hunt Club Room, The Sorrento will be an all-consuming evening affair.

NOTE: The rooms at The Sorrento are undergoing a face-lift, and the gray, masculine feeling of the suites is being replaced with more elegant appointments in soft pastel colors.

"BHY" KRACKE PARK

Take Fifth Avenue north from downtown to Highland Drive on southeast Queen Anne Hill. The park is at the intersection of Fifth Avenue and Highland. It is also known as Comstock Park.

Unless you read the original version of **Best Places To Kiss,** or live in this neighborhood, you probably won't know this park with the funny name even exists. As you drive through the unpretentious neighborhood setting, you'll probably think nothing of the small, unobtrusive playground on your left. But wait, stop and take another look.

"Bhy" Kracke Park starts off as an innocent playground less than a block long, at the bottom of a hill. On either side of it, landscaped walkways begin angling upwards, meet, curve around and up and around and up, to the top of the hill. And in that is the payoff: five tiers of thick miniature leas with strategically placed park benches and densely vined pathways leading to a startling city view. Around each turn is another city-glimpse, creating a buildup for what lies at the top. When you get there you'll exclaim simultaneously, *"This is unbelievable!"*

NOTE: If you don't want to walk up, drive to the entrance on Comstock at the top of the hill and walk down one tier.

HIGHLAND DRIVE

From Roy Street in Queen Anne, turn onto the steep part of Queen Anne Avenue North. Two blocks up, turn left on West Highland Drive and follow it along the southwestern slope of the hill.

This street, lined with mansions and classic older apartment buildings, sits with a prominent southwestern view below the summit of Queen Anne Hill. The drive through this exclusive neighborhood with grand, detailed views of the city and Sound peaks when you reach the intersection of Seventh West, Eighth Place West and West Highland. In front of you is a grassy knoll with benches from which there's one of the most sweeping, complete views of the Sound to be had, with the islands south and west and a full Olympic skyline. This area is more like an excerpt from a storybook, it is that picturesque. With a picnic snack in tow, you can spend an entire summer afternoon up here in each other's arms.

THE BYZANTION

806 East Roy, Seattle 98112
(206) 325-7580
Inexpensive to Very Reasonable

Take Broadway Street north through the Capitol Hill district to East Roy Street and turn west. The Byzantion is on the north side of the street across from the Harvard Exit movie theatre.

Seattle's Broadway district has nothing to match the neon blaze its New York counterpart has, yet this diminutive replica (minus the theatres), with boutiques, cafes and restaurants, is a magnet for the uptown, new age and punkophile types of the city, not to exclude the more ordinary types like myself who also come here. A walk down this 1/2-mile of glitzy variety can be fun and educational for anyone in the mood to browse the shops and watch the people.

After you've had your fill, duck onto East Roy at the north end of Broadway. Hidden there, away from all the madness, is this demure, cozy Greek restaurant that personifies intimate dining. The room is awash in low, golden candlelight regardless of the time of day. Romanesque murals cover the walls in soft, earthen tones. The dishes are mostly traditional Greek and are thoroughly rich, succulent and impressive. There are also vegetarian dishes available. Plus, the service is patient and unusually caring.

NOTE: The restaurant serves a health-aware breakfast and Sunday brunch of whole-wheat pancakes and waffles with fresh roasted coffee and fresh-squeezed juices.

LAKE UNION BED & BREAKFAST❤❤❤❤

2217 North 36th Street, Seattle 98103
(206) 547-9965
Incredibly Moderate to Expensive

Call for reservations and directions.

This bed & breakfast comes recommended only with a twofold warning: First, even if you have good directions and know Seattle, the home is a trick to find (so be sure to ask for the business names that front this location). Second, when you do finally locate the address and walk inside you'll want the owners to move out so you can move in.

The home is an impressive, three-story wood building looking out over the north end of Lake Union. You enter it through a landscaped garden of trees enclosed by a 6-foot-tall brick wall. The modest-sized interior has thick white carpeting, and in the living room just off the hallways, overstuffed white chairs surround a marble fireplace. Upon arrival hors d'oeuvres and champagne laced with Chambord liqueur or a prize-winning wine await your sampling.

The B&B accommodates two couples, on the house's second floor. The penthouse is a huge room dressed in willow tree furniture with a fireplace of brown marble. The bathroom has a large Jacuzzi with a superb view of the lake and city, and there are control-heated tile floors that run into the sun-drenched solarium, which has the same wonderful view. The other upstairs bedroom, which is much less expensive, is simple and comfortable and has a private bathroom located a distance away down on the main floor. That would automatically be a romantic no-no if the bathroom didn't contain a glass-brick-enclosed sauna, piped-in music and a large tiled shower. Oh yes, and the breakfast: a superlative seven-course culinary presentation of souffles, pastries, lattes, fruits, granola, egg dishes and anything else the owner/chef creates, served on Lenox china and Baccarat crystal. After all that, I feel safe in stating that this is the best place to kiss in Seattle whether you're eating, sleeping, standing or lounging!

◆ **THE BEST ROMANTIC OPTION:** Upon request, the eccentric and brilliant owner/chef of the house, who has a *Type A* gourmand personality, will prepare a dinner feast for you in the home if you're staying there, the likes of which you can taste only at her restaurant, **Teger's, 2302 24th Avenue East, Seattle, (206) 324-3373** (Somewhat Reasonable to Very Moderate). The restaurant is open just Wednesday through Saturday (one seating only), and then only when the chef is in town. For an extra-intimate touch, call Teger's ahead of time and describe the meal of your dreams and it can be served to you that evening; or, on the nights the restaurant is closed, you may make the same request at the bed & breakfast, whether or not you're spending the night.

OPTIMUM SEAFARE RESTAURANT

5509 University Way, Seattle 98105
(206) 527-1033
Expensive

Ten blocks north of the center of the University District on University Way.

In a section of the University District you wouldn't think even remotely romantic sits a modestly converted house-turned-health-conscious-gourmet restaurant. The interior is softly lit and has a very intimate, quiet feel and eclectic, homey motif. Here you can feast on an epicurean dinner brimming with the freshest seafood imaginable. This restaurant is to Northwest dining what the Olympics are to the Northwest landscape. The meals are lovingly prepared and eagerly presented by knowledgeable and attentive waitpeople. Salads may be adorned with violets, fresh water chestnuts and creative dressings. The fish is succulent, with such sauces as a Ghana peanut glaze or tangy Cuban black-bean marinade. With the last sip of sherry served as a finishing touch, you easily slip into the blissful satisfaction that accompanies such a dining event.

NOTE: Service can be slow, which for some diners is a drawback but for others is the only way to dine. The food is always worth the wait.

MAGNOLIA BOULEVARD

Take Elliott Avenue to the Magnolia Bridge, take the bridge and stay to your left. At the first stop sign turn left and follow Magnolia Boulevard for approximately three miles.

Magnolia Boulevard snakes around the edge of the Magnolia area of Seattle. This urban borough is blessed by a majestic 180-degree view of the Sound. The cliffs along its southwest border showcase an overview of the city and Olympics that can motivate avid feelings of the heart.

As you follow the drive, you will notice several obvious places to pull off and park. The panoramas from these areas are spectacular, but unfortunately, no privacy is afforded there. However, if you walk from the grass-lined curb down to the edge of the cliff overlooking the water, the street is no longer visible. Here is your private corner of the world to, side by side, watch sunset making its final performance of the day.

NOTE: A wool blanket will help make the damp grass more comfortable.

DISCOVERY PARK SAND CLIFFS

The park is in northwest Magnolia. To enter the park from Magnolia Boulevard, take the Magnolia Bridge exit off Elliott Avenue and stay to your left. At the first stop sign turn left onto Magnolia Boulevard and follow it till it dead-ends at the Park's southeast entrance.

Discovery Park is one of my favorite neighborhood parks. This isn't just any ordinary Northwest park, so don't let the generic name dissuade you from traveling out here. It is an unusual area with a variety of trails and terrain: Hike through dense woods or along sandy cliffs above the Sound where there's unmarred exposure to everything due north, south and west. Or take the wooden steps leading down to the shore and linger among driftwood, rocks and beach-life.

While wandering through your new romantic *discovery* (pun intended), look for the sand cliffs on the southwest side of the park. During the winter, when sundown occurs in the late afternoon, you will find these golden, interwoven hills an intoxicating vantage point for watching the passing of day into an early night.

NOTE: Except for at the height of summer, dress warmly and wear a windbreaker. No matter how much you cuddle, the breeze up here will send a chill through your sweaters.

HOT-AIR BALLOONING

There are several balloon companies in the Seattle area and in other areas of the Northwest and Southwest Canada. Check the yellow pages for the one nearest you.

If you're thinking that a hot-air-balloon ride sounds like a frivolous, expensive, childlike excursion to embark on, you're right, that's exactly what it is, a Mary Poppins liftoff into fantasy-land. A morning balloon ride will tingle and excite in a way that surpasses your wildest expectations of what hovering silently above the ground is like.

Usually you depart at sunrise. Your first impression will be astonishment at the enormous mass of billowing material overhead and the dragon fire that fills it with air. As you step into the gondola your heart will begin to flutter with expectation. Once aloft, as the wind guides your craft above the countryside, the world will appear more peaceful than you ever thought possible. You will also be startled at the splendor of sunrise from way up here as daylight awakens the mountains with fresh color and warmth.

Some balloon companies will provide brunch or champagne and pastries after your flight. This is the time to discuss how being carried away has suddenly taken on a new meaning, which the two of you will keep in your hearts forever. A caress while floating over the world on a cloudless summer day can be a thoroughly heavenly experience.

"Don't miss love, it's an incredible gift."
Leo F. Buscaglia

The above listings are arranged alphabetically. The following descriptions are arranged geographically north to south.

THE OREGON COAST

It is probably safe to say that no other state has a span of highway quite like Highway 101 in Oregon. This road hugs the entire length of the coast and most every magnificent mile has consistent visual contact with the scenery. The drive is, in a word, breathtaking. Thank goodness there are enough turnoffs, vistas, parks, hikes, undiscovered coves, rocky inlets and ravines to stop for so you can drink in the view at your own leisurely pace.

The only concern you need be aware of is that this area is constant witness to the temperamental mood swings of the weather. At times the mixture of fog and sea moisture create a diffuse screen through which this world appears as an apparition in a mist. Other moments bring a disturbing quiet as a tempest brews in the distance, where ocean and sky meet and bond as one. Yet, even on the calmest of summer days, the unbridled energy and siren-song of the waves unleashing their power against beaches, headlands and haystack rocks creates an impact that is spellbinding. Once visited, the Oregon Coast will remain a poignant memory for rekindling your relationship with each other and the world.

NOTE: For information on parks and recreation areas call (503) 378-6305 or (503) 842-4981.

CANNON BEACH

Cannon Beach is west just off of Highway 101. Take Highway 26 from Portland west to Highway 101 and head south to Cannon Beach. Highway 30 from the north will also access Highway 101.

As you approach Cannon Beach it will be hard to believe your eyes — the exhilarating scope of the infinite procession of cliffs and ocean. There are over seven miles of beach here — with firm sand and rolling waves that beckon dreamers and those in love to don wet suits and ride the curl into shore.

The seascape is crowded with massive outcroppings and island-rocks, the hallmarks of this coastline. Special to Cannon Beach is a freestanding monolith that is indeed a natural wonder, called Haystack Rock, the third largest of its kind in the world. At low tide you can stand at its threshold and feel humbled by its towering dimensions.

The nickname for the entire Oregon Coast is the Sunset Empire, and a more succinct title does not exist. As the sun begins to settle into the ocean, the brilliant colors radiate from the horizon, filling the sky like a golden aurora borealis. At first the light penetrates the clouds as a pale lavender-blue haze, transforming suddenly to an intense yellow-amber, culminating in a fiery red that seems to set the sky on fire. Then, as dusk finalizes its entrance, the clouds fade to steel blue-grey and the sky changes its countenance from cobalt blue to indigo. Slowly, the moon takes a central place in the evening heavens, reflecting its presence on the surface of the water in rays of platinum. When the weather is cooperating, this entertainment takes place nightly on Cannon Beach and the entire Oregon Coast.

♦ **ROMANTIC OPTIONS: Ecola State Park** and **Indian Beach** are just to the north of Cannon Beach off Highway 101. State parks are rarely good places to kiss in. Though they may be well-kept and just as supreme as anywhere else, they also tend to be crowded, inundated with RVs and kids, which can diminish the appeal of your surroundings. Yet, due to the exceptional character of this area, the potency of the sights are likely to blur whoever else may be around you, except each other.

ROMANTIC WARNING: On a warm summer day Cannon Beach is one crowded area, with traffic and congestion like you wouldn't believe. Consider the quiet town of Oceanside (described in this section), another hour's drive down the coast, as an alternative to the potential mobs here.

THE ARGONAUTA INN

P.O. Box 3, Cannon Beach 97110
(503) 436-2601
Reasonable to Expensive

In Cannon Beach, turn west off Highway 101 onto Sunset. Drive to Hemlock Street and turn south. At First Street turn west and then south again at Larch. The Argonauta Inn is to the right of the dead-end.

This eclectic, imaginative arrangement of rose-colored suites, a Victorian cottage and a beach house is set right at the center of everything Cannon Beach has to offer. The beach is at your front door and the town is at your back. Glass-enclosed patios, fireplaces, complete kitchens, antiques, powerful panoramas combined with homey touches make this one of the most interesting places to stay. It's definitely the most original and provocative.

NOTE: The beach house has three large bedrooms that three couples could nicely share for a joint outing that could be playfully romantic and considerably less money per couple.

THE HEARTSTONE INN

P.O. Box 66, Tolvana Park 97145
(503) 436-2266
Off-Season/Reasonable; On-Season/Moderate

From Highway 101 turn off onto the Beach Loop Road passing through Cannon Beach into Tolvana Park. The Inn is at the intersection of Hemlock and Jackson streets.

For a coastal change of pace, particularly if the summer pace of the beach is a bit much for you, and you want to be near the surf, but not quite that near, the Heartstone Inn is your answer. In an out-of-the-way corner of Tolvana Park, this unobtrusive, contemporary wood building, sheltered in the local beach community and hidden by gently swaying willow trees, looks more like a residence than it does a lodging. Yet there are four generous studios inside, with vaulted cedar ceilings, beach-rock fireplaces, skylights and stained glass windows. The beach is a short walk away and accessible for an invigorating morning walk on compact, damp sand, along the ocean calm of low tide. All of this combines to create a refreshingly private and welcome place to stay.

OSWALD WEST STATE PARK

*Ten miles south of Cannon Beach on the west side of Highway 101 is the
entrance to the park. Look for the signs pointing the way.*

Oswald West State Park is one of the most ideal, inspiring
campgrounds in these parts, just ask any Northwest camping
enthusiast. Its superior desirability to most other campsites has to do
with inaccessibility. In order to set up, you need to walk 1/4-mile
down a path through a forest, wheeling a cart they provide with your
things piled on top. This short jaunt tends to separate out the serious
campers from the featherweights. Besides giving you that much-
needed privacy, the park resides in a forested setting within arm's
reach of the water. There are adjacent paths that take you briskly
down to the pounding surf. The scenery to the south manifests a
succession of overlapping mountains jutting out into the ocean,
culminating in a dark jagged profile against the distant skyline. The
white sand, effervescent surf and rock-clad shore make exploring a
treasure-hunt-like game only two can play.

OCEANSIDE

Much of the Oregon Coast is heavily traveled, especially in the summer — except, that is, for Oceanside. This remote location is about eight miles west from the main road on the small peninsula that creates Tillamook Bay. The drive along this section of the coast, separating you from the crowds, affords you plenty of opportunities to stop whenever you see an inviting stretch of rugged coastline to run along together, utterly alone . . . Rummage through a rocky crevasse, dig for clams and listen to the rhapsody of the ocean from a forested cliff. At the end of your well-spent day, a light fog may shroud the shore as you circle down a road toward the village of Oceanside. As the mist mingles with the cry of sea life, you will know for sure that you've left city life behind you, far, far away.

There is nothing fancy in Oceanside; the handful of accommodations range from basic to austere, and there are only two restaurants in the area. But the untouched, concinnous Oregon coastline is the reason to be here, with only yourselves and the calm of the moment to concern you.

♦ *ROMANTIC POSSIBILITIES:* **Roseanna's Restaurant, Oceanside 97134, (503) 842-7351** (Reasonable to Moderate), is Oceanside's only *oceanside* restaurant. Healthy morning breakfasts, lunches and dinners begin by first offering the appetizer of a window-framed ocean panorama. A dinner coinciding with the sunset will finish the day with a dessert prepared by nature.

THREE CAPES SCENIC LOOP

Before Tillamook you will see signs for the Three Capes Scenic Loop. After you turn west off of Highway 101, continue following the signs along this loop to Cape Meares, around and south to Oceanside and then down to Netarts.

Highway 101 does consistently offer traveling companions beautiful things to gaze at and admire. Unfortunately, even though 101 isn't a superhighway, the tendency is to drive fast or be subject to nasty looks from those having to slow up behind you. The only time you can safely reduce speed is when you enter a town's shopping area and the traffic forces you to comply, and then there's nothing to see.

You can avoid all this pressure on the Three Capes Scenic Loop. Even on the sunniest day in summer the throngs of tourists seem to be somewhere else and your movement along this exquisite passage through forest and ocean beaches is at any pace you choose. You can stop at dozens of locations to dig for clams or go crabbing. **Anderson Viewpoint,** a precipitous mountain bluff just south of Oceanside that overlooks everything north, south and west, is an unparalleled location for a picnic. When your day's journey is done, you can collapse into each other's arms and reminisce about the images you've enjoyed.

THREE CAPES BED & BREAKFAST ❦❧❦❧

1685 Maxwell Mountain Road, Oceanside 97134
(503) 842-6126
Inexpensive

From Tillamook, take Third Street, west. Follow the signs to Netarts and
Oceanside. In Oceanside follow the shoreline on Pacific Avenue. Turn
right at the stop sign, then left at the sign indicating Maxwell Mountain Road.

This is not a fancy bed & breakfast. Yet, the effect of the
encompassing landscape from the bay windows of your homespun
room can make any morning or sunset seem a dream come true. The
home is situated on the side of a hill overlooking the spectacular
Oceanside shore. One of the rooms has a private deck and private
entrance. Not exactly Nirvana, but then again, it depends on what
you make of it.

♦ **ROMANTIC OPTION:** Up the road from Three Capes Bed
& Breakfast is an interesting set of gray, weathered buildings with a
huge sign plastered on one side reading, "Motel." This tackily
advertised accommodation goes by the name of **House On The Hill,
Oceanside 97134, (503) 842-6030** (Very Reasonable). The *hill* is
in reality one of the highest points along the entire coast, and the
views from the motel rooms, through floor-to-ceiling windows, are
nothing less than startling. Sadly, the interiors are nothing less than
early tacky, but they are clean and, well, there isn't much else around.
There definitely isn't a better view around for the money, anywhere.

CHEZ JEANETTE

7150 Old Gleneden Highway, Gleneden Beach 97388
(503) 764-3434
Expensive

From Lincoln City take Highway 101 three miles south to the Gleneden junction where you turn west onto old Highway 101. Chez Jeanette is 1/4-mile down the road, the first house on the east side.

This restaurant would delight the most finicky of gourmands. Chez Jeanette is a divinely elegant place that has a reclusive hobbit-like aura about it. The stone-fronted, homey structure is snug against a vine-covered hill and has thick branches curling around its roof and walls. The entrance is a formal oak door with a small, steel-girded peephole a bit too near the top for the average hobbit to find useful.

The small dining salon is warmed by two blazing fireplaces that illuminate the softly lit room. Velvety forest-green drapery, lush carpet, regal chairs and wood tables set with bone china and crystal create an atmosphere that satisfies your eyes. After you finish the delectable, creative meal, the rest of you will be satisfied as well. Chez Jeanette's provocative decor, location, intriguing menu and excellent service make it a restaurant for romance and discreet hobbit-watching.

CHANNEL HOUSE

P.O. Box 56, Depoe Bay, Oregon 97369
(503) 765-2140
Expensive

In Depoe Bay on Highway 101 look for the signs on the west side of the road for Channel House, which will direct you to turn west onto Ellingson Street. At the dead-end is the House.

Don't let the street entrance to Channel House fool you or disappoint you — another existence awaits once you're inside with your door closed. Appropriately named, this towering bed & breakfast sits above the volatile entrance to Depoe Bay. The rocky-cliff setting and venerable coastline are visible from most every room. Some of the more desirable rooms (read expensive) have their own private deck, where the steaming hot Jacuzzi is a way to kick back and let go, while you watch the boat traffic file by.

The view and hot tub are two reasons for a secluded stay here; another is the handsome, oversized suites that ooze comfort and relaxation. Sit back and let the fireplace warm the sea air and melt the stress of the week away.

OCEAN HOUSE BED & BREAKFAST ✦✦✦✦

4920 N.W. Woody Way, Newport 97365
(503) 265-6158
Reasonable to Moderate

Call or write for reservations and directions.

If you find yourselves at Ocean House Bed & Breakfast, either on a warm summer day or during a storm blowing in from the north, your child-like curiosities and excitement will quickly find their way to the surface and want to stay. Perched atop Agate Beach, with a huge lawn and garden through which runs a private trail down to the beach, this B&B provides plenty of space for stretching out and searching the shore for whatever may be there to find. The windows of the bedrooms upstairs open toward the sea, the downstairs room opens to an outside deck. Superior standards of comfort and care have been upheld over two decades at this sizable country home. Your chance to experience Ocean House for yourselves is closer than you think.

STARFISH POINT

140 N.W. 48th Street, Newport 97365
(503) 265-3751
Expensive

Call for reservations and directions.

Starfish Point used to be a development of time-share con-
dominium-like units that didn't quite make it on the time-share
circuit, and on first glance the ordinary, natural wood buildings that
look more suburban than country seem to explain why. On closer
inspection, it becomes a mystery why someone wouldn't want to
spend time here. Starfish Point is down the road a piece from Ocean
House, on the same cliff with the same back yard view. Each unit is
outfitted with two large bedrooms, a designer kitchen, a study lined
with bay windows, fireplace, fair-sized Jacuzzi for two in the master
bath, stereo and TV, and units 4, 5 and 6 have superb views. If luxury
without room service suits you, this is assuredly one of your better
options on the coast, and there's enough room so you can share it
with another fun-loving couple and split the cost.

THE OREGON HOUSE

94288 Highway 101, Yachats 97498
(503) 547-3329
Very Inexpensive to Reasonable

Just north of Yachats, directly off of Highway 101 on the west side of the
road.

This is one difficult kissing place to explain because it is so sprawling
and still in the stages of being renovated by its new owners. First,
there are seven very diverse rooms here, some with rambling,
family-oriented floor plans, others with just one comfortable room
overlooking well-kept grounds and a distant piercing blue ocean.
Each unit, regardless of size, includes an assortment of the following:
fireplace, skylight, dining nook, deck, patio and full utilitarian
kitchen. Now, none of that is particularly exceptional, but when you
take into consideration the oceanside landscape of rolling lawn
heading down to the windswept beach below, the price, and how
the new owners have greatly improved the place over the past year,
the Oregon House actually is shaping up to be one distinctive place
to stay.

♦ **ROMANTIC OPTION: La Serre Restaurant, Second &**
Beach Street, Yachats 97498, (503) 547-3420 (Moderate), is a
welcome reprieve along a coastline where most restaurants are either
formal or American-standard. La Serre is a refined, gourmet dining
experience with a heavy emphasis on natural, fresh whole foods. The
interior emphasizes the organic with thriving greenery, oak tables
and a wood floor. This is the place where a meal will tend to your
palate, health awareness and need to be close all at the same time.

CHARLESTON STATE PARKS

The town of Charleston is southwest of Coos Bay on a small peninsula 30 miles due west of Highway 101. The trio of state parks south of town are well-marked and well worth the detour from the main road. They are unrivaled in their varied perspectives and contrasts given that they are separated by only a few miles.

The first park is **Sunset Bay,** where forest and cool sandy earth flank a small inlet of calm ocean water. The second, farther south, is **Shore Acres.** The remains of an estate, this park is renowned for its enormous formal gardens, which are maintained to resemble their former glory, and its crowning location on a soaring cliff high above Oregon's coast. There are numerous lookouts and intriguing paths that ramble over rock-strewn beaches gouged with caves and granite fissures where the water releases its energy in spraying foam and crashing waves. The third park, **Cape Arago,** has less imposing grounds and is more of an everyday picnic spot than its neighbors to the north, except for its disposition high above the shoreline with a northern view of the coast. It is known for its sea lions and harbor seals romping in the surf or sleeping languidly on the rocks.

HILL HOUSE BED & BREAKFAST ❤❤❤❤

P.O. Box 1428, Bandon-by-the-Sea 97411
(503) 347-2678
Moderate

Call for reservations and directions.

Bandon-by-the-Sea is one of a few relatively undiscovered seaside towns along the Oregon Coast. Yet the beach here is more spectacular and interesting than at any of the more popular sites. The multitude of haystack rocks that rise in tiers from the ocean are literally awesome. For those yearning for a sanctuary away from the usual, this small community on the water is your exact answer.

The Hill House has two gracious, homey guest-rooms that permit a communion with the ocean rarely found indoors. The House's choice location on Bandon's splendid shoreline facilitates this personal interaction, with the wide sand-beach being part of your front yard. A large deck wraps around the front of the home and is a perfect place to snuggle together over morning espresso as you watch the tide dance across the rocks and shore. The breakfast that follows will be a delicious prelude to the day ahead. Bandon and Hill House can be a soothing answer for much-needed time alone together.

♦ **ROMANTIC SUGGESTION:** The most romantic dining for miles around is the **Inn at Face Rock, 3225 Beach Loop Drive, Bandon 97411, (503) 347-9441** (Moderate). The solarium dining room has a distant view of the water and the food is good — the fish sometimes outstanding.

SCENE-HOPPING SUGGESTIONS: Start at **The Argonauta** in the heart of Cannon Beach, preferably in the beginning of the week when the area is more quiet. After a day or two continue down the coast for a night at **Three Capes Bed & Breakfast** and have a sunset dinner at **Roseanna's Restaurant** in Oceanside. Farther down, a night at the **Channel House** soaking in the hot tub out on your private deck will keep your thoughts and body warm for a long, lovely evening. You can end your holiday with a quiet day on Agate Beach residing at the **Ocean House Bed & Breakfast**.

> *"He gave her a look you could have spread on a waffle."*
>
> Ring Lardner

T H E   C A S C A D E S

The places above are listed alphabetically. The following descriptions are arranged geographically, north to south from the Gorge to Ashland.

COLUMBIA RIVER GORGE

Oregon's Interstate Highway 84 borders the south side of the Columbia River. Highway 14 runs parallel to it on the north side of the river in Washington state. There are several bridges across the river between Oregon and Washington.

The Columbia River Gorge is a very appropriate entry for this kissing travelogue. The 60 miles or so of scenery formed by the river carving its way through the Cascade mountains is a kaleidoscope of heart-stirring images. To travel this passage is to come face to face with an area where magic is afoot in the emerald mountains on the west, and blazened across the sun-burnt mountains and grasslands to the east. This is a vast collage of all the intensely beautiful things the Northwest has to offer.

Embellished by the folk tales and Indian mythology native to these parts, the scads of falls, ponds, mountain lakes, hikes and wonderful vistas all fashion the Gorge's personality. But the waterfalls are undoubtedly the most remarkable natural feature. Depending on the season, they rush to earth in a variety of contours and intensities: Oneonta Falls drops abruptly off a sheer ledge for several hundred feet. Elowah Falls sprays a fine, showery mist over deciduous forest. Punch Bowl Falls pours into crystal clear Eagle Creek. Upper Horsetail Falls is forced out in a jet stream through a portal centered in a wall of rock and Wahkeenah Falls rushes over rocky steps and beds of stone. But wherever you happen to be in the Columbia River Gorge, its stunning natural pageantry will feel a little like paradise regained.

THE COLUMBIA RIVER SCENIC HIGHWAY 💋

The 22-mile route starts at the Ainsworth Park exit or the Troutdale exit on I-84 east of Portland.

This highway, constructed in 1915, is reported to be an engineering classic. It is also said that this scenic route was the first paved road to cross the Cascades. Though all that's certainly true, once you drive this sinuous, moss-covered work of art, you will swear it was really built by wizards. As you round every turn, you'll be pleased to see the integrity of the past is intact and remains so for almost the entire drive. You won't be bothered by neon, billboards, superhighways, traffic signs or speeding cars. This road accentuates the scenery. In the days when it was built, driving was called touring and cars moseyed along at 30 miles an hour. You can go a tad faster through here now, but not much, and why bother — you won't want to miss the falls, hikes and roadside vistas that show up suddenly along the way.

NOTE: During summer, when kids are out of school, this can be a very crowded strip of road. The best romantic time is when school is in session.

◆ **ROMANTIC OPTION:** I do not like recommending tourist attractions. The crowds usually prevent intimate moments or any privacy whatsoever. The restaurant in the **Multnomah Falls Lodge, Bridal Veil 97010, (503) 695-2376** (Moderate) is indeed a tourist attraction, and if it weren't for one unbelievable feature (proclaimed in the Lodge's name), this would be just another Northwest wood-and-stone dining room serving three decent meals a day. That attraction, of course, is a plummeting waterfall, spilling for a dramatic 620 feet, almost in the Lodge's back yard. This spectacle makes any snack or meal here a momentous occasion.

COLUMBIA GORGE HOTEL
RESTAURANT

4000 West Cliff Drive, Hood River 97031
(503) 386-5566
Very Expensive

One hour east of Portland on Interstate 84, take exit 62 to the hotel.

The wide-ranging grounds of this nostalgic, Spanish-styled villa are on a high, forested bank of the Columbia River with Mount Hood's glacial peak peering through in the distance. The atmosphere is reminiscent of an elegant 1920's country estate, with crystal, silver, pastel tablecloths and arched bay windows looking over the woods and river.

If you plan on being in the neighborhood, make certain your schedule includes a morning stop here. Then: Get ready for a breakfast extravaganza. From pancakes to biscuits, fresh fruit, eggs and everything in between, this is the same gargantuan breakfast served at the Snoqualmie Falls Lodge in Washington state. This meal is guaranteed to appease every taste bud you possess (and you'll discover some you didn't know about). It is strongly recommended that you prepare yourselves for it the night before . . . How you prepare is up to you.

◆ **ROMANTIC OPTION:** Rather than staying in the rooms of the Columbia Gorge Hotel, which are outrageously overpriced and in need of remodeling, consider the **Barkheimer House, 3820 West Cliff Drive, Hood River 97031, (503) 386-5918** (Moderate), only a half-mile down the road from the hotel. This largish country home has a wide deck overlooking the river and Gorge, old-fashioned, comfortable rooms with stone fireplaces and a hearty breakfast, making it an easy place to call home at a more moderate price.

TIMBERLINE LODGE

Timberline 97028
(503) 226-7979; Out-Of-State, (800) 547-1406;
In Oregon, (800) 452-1335
Moderate to Expensive

Traveling to Mount Hood from the south, follow Highway 26 up the east side of the mountain. As you near the summit, turn onto Timberline Access road, which will take you to the Lodge. From Portland, go east on Highway 26 to Government Camp, where the Timberline Access road starts its six-mile climb to the Lodge.

Mount Hood, like its relative to the north, Mount Rainier, stands as an overpowering display of nature's potency and abandoned genius. Appropriately, near the summit there rests a design of human creativity, Timberline Lodge.

This grand structure is endowed with character and masterful craftsmanship, evidenced in its metal filigree, brick chimneys, steepled rooftops and carved beams. The interior strap-metal furniture, wall murals and intricately arranged wood rafters are further testimony to this artistry. Originally built in 1937, the rooms are beautifully restored, each having an inviting, comfortable decor; some with fireplaces. This handsome Lodge and captivating Mount Hood together create a scene of rugged romance perfect for two.

NOTE: In winter, when snow transforms the area into a winter wonderland, the Lodge's toastiness and the rush of downhill or cross-country skiing make this a sensationally sensual hideaway.

INN AT COOPER SPUR

10755 Cooper Spur Road, Mount Hood 97041
(503) 352-6037
Moderate to Expensive

*Take Highway 26 to Government Camp, where you access Highway 35
to Hood River. Nineteen miles past Government Camp, before you reach
Hood River, turn left onto Cooper Spur Road. Follow it 2 1/4-miles to
the Inn.*

This restaurant is best described as a romantic anomaly. It definitely
has all the outward signs of a provincial mountain snuggery: At the
foot of a gentle slope, a log gateway guards a stone path leading to
a distinguished wood and stucco chalet exterior. Inside there is more
distinctive woodwork, and the aroma of just-baked pies solicitously
dances about the room. Who could deny how quaint and cozy all
that sounds? And it is, but only to a point. What you discover is
that the interior's homey contents and laid-back atmosphere really
make this more a place for hiking or ski chums than a haven for
starry-eyed lovers. Nevertheless, though this may not exactly be the
esoteric destination you were looking for, the Inn at Cooper Spur
has mountain hospitality aplenty and a more social kind of fun.

NOTE: The owners of the Inn have been slowly turning this place
into a resort complete with cabins and a main lodge. It is an alternative
to Timberline, but only if you can't get a room up there.

ROCK SPRINGS GUEST RANCH ❖❖❖❖

64201 Tyler Road, Bend 97701
(503) 382-1957
Moderate to Expensive

On Highway 20 head toward the small town of Tumalo 10 miles north of Bend. Immediately after you pass the town of Tumalo, look for the signs that direct you to the Ranch.

Ever since I visited Rock Springs Guest Ranch I have secretly longed to return. The memories of my time there are crystal clear, and when I recall the serenity I came to know during my stay, I feel a silent euphoria.

My first impression of the Ranch came as I drove up the dusty dirt road toward it and saw a grassy meadow full of vigorous horses playing rambunctiously. It was obvious that I had either truly found the Ponderosa or these were the type of horses you could look at but not touch. I'm a city woman born and raised and my experience with horses has been from riding stables, where the animals look like they would rather die than be touched one more time by human hands. At Rock Springs, nothing could be further from that urban reality. These horses adored human contact. They were eager to be tended to and even more eager to challenge the trails and paths that covered the countryside.

To adequately portray this diamond-in-the-rough location I should probably describe the arresting scenery of mountains and rambling streams or elaborately detail the accommodations of cabins with fireplaces and large outdoor hot tub and swimming pool . . . But the essence of the Ranch is not revealed by such details; rather, it is in the reverent feeling instilled in the heart as you traverse this land on horseback with someone you love, the breeze cooling your brow in fall and spring, the blush of winter cold on your cheeks, or the balmy summer sun tanning your face while an eagle soars overhead. All represent your stay here at Rock Springs.

As soon as I can get my hands on a parcel of time with my significant other, my saddle bags will be packed and I will return to one of the most inspiring escapes I found in the Northwest.

NOTE: The environment at the Ranch, especially during the summer, is family oriented. Plan a visit when school is in session for the optimal romantic atmosphere. Also the meals are served family style in the main lodge and are included in the package price.

ASHLAND

Ashland, Oregon, is a world unto itself — tranquil neighborhoods, exciting town center, cosmopolitan nightlife, rural countryside, mountainous terrain bordering river valleys — all, amazingly, located out in the middle of nowhere. Not only is the location absolutely stunning and the numerous accommodations literally among the best the Northwest has to offer, but the theatre season, beginning in February and running through October, makes New York City's Broadway pale by comparison. It will take only one visit to make both of you sustaining members of Ashland's annual Shakespeare Festival. Before you scoff, keep in mind that the Shakespeare plays are only a portion of each season's theatrical options.

THE LOCATION: You need not understand the sundry geographical patterns that constitute the Cascades to be fascinated by the radical change in landscape you'll behold as you head south along the western edge of the mountains down to Ashland. At first, the differences will be disconcerting, especially in summer. Without warning, the lofty, dense-green forests of the west are replaced by the rolling desert hills and parched terrain of the sun-drenched east. The colors of this horizon are shades of tan, ash and gold in undulating gradations and intensities. In summer Mount Ashland's parched peak looming over the town and California's Mount Shasta in the distance, framed by eroded hills, create the perfect motif for a Wild West movie.

THE TOWN: The remarkable thing about Ashland is that there is more to do in this small, quaint town than in most any city in the Northwest. There are: white-water rafting down the Rogue or Klamath rivers, horseback riding, parks, shops, restaurants, art galleries, jazz concerts, a symphony orchestra, llama hikes, mountain climbing and, during the winter, downhill and cross-country skiing minutes away on Mount Ashland. It's unbelievable, but it's there for the enjoying. I cannot think of a more diversified getaway anywhere in the Northwest — or U.S. for that matter — than Ashland for a honeymoon, anniversary or just being together.

◆ **ROMANTIC OPTION:** In the heart of the theatre district is **Lithia Rose Park,** consisting of 100 acres of lawn, forest, ponds, trails, tennis courts, flower gardens, volleyball court and enough space that a portion of this lovely tiered playground can be yours.

SOARING HAWKS

P.O. Box 944, Ashland 97520
(503) 482-8707
For two of you/Expensive — For two couples/Reasonable

Please call for information regarding reservations and directions.

This was the only kissing place where the owners tried to talk me out of including a description in this book. Their "secluded mountain home" was so precious to them that they didn't want everyone to know about it. I assured them that the readers of **The Best Places To Kiss** were a special type of traveler, looking for places they could cherish and not ravage. That promise made, I am thrilled to describe to you one of the absolute BEST places to kiss in the Northwest.

The home is an octagonal wood masterpiece, jutting out from the forested slopes of Mount Ashland, poised over an unparalleled 180-degree view of the Cascade and Siskiyou mountains, and Mount Shasta 70 miles to the south. Special features of the house include a vaulted living room ceiling with a gigantic rock fireplace, floor-to-ceiling windows, a hot tub, a bi-level deck encompassing the entire abode and top-notch bedrooms with peerless comforts and that priceless view. Located only 16 miles from downtown Ashland and two miles from the ski slopes, the best of all worlds is available at Soaring Hawks.

NOTE: A minimum three-day stay is required. Also, during the winter the driveway to the front door is impassable so a 400-foot walk through snow is inescapable, but worth the trouble.

♦ **ROMANTIC ALTERNATIVE:** In the event that Soaring Hawks is booked, inquire into staying down the road a bit at the **Mount Ashland Inn, 550 Mt. Ashland Road, Ashland 97520, (503) 482-8707** (Moderate). This bed & breakfast was designed and built by the same people who created Soaring Hawks. The Inn has smaller rooms and the view is less praiseworthy. But it is less expensive and you are indeed up in the mountains in the heart of the Pacific Crest Trail (the Inn is built directly next to the Trail). The breakfast is wonderful, each room has a private bath and the log structure is close to the finest in mountain accommodations. Not at all a bad option for a bit of mountain intimacy.

ROMEO INN BED & BREAKFAST⬥⬥⬥⬥

295 Idaho Street, Ashland 97520
(503) 488-0884
Expensive

From Ashland's main plaza head south on Main Street and turn right onto Gresham Street. Two blocks down turn left on Holly and then left on Idaho. The inn is on the corner of Idaho and Holly.

I almost decided to drive right by this one and not check it out. The area was far from being a place I would want to spend loving moments in. Once you're inside though, the outside melts away and the two of you have all the elements of a romantic interlude: large, sophisticated, country-style rooms; a swimming pool encompassed by a well-tended garden; a generous, conscientiously prepared breakfast. The Stratford Suite and the Canterbury Room will be of particular interest to those who want a fireplace, hot tub and private entrance.

COWSLIP'S BELLE

159 N. Main Street, Ashland 97520
(503) 488-2901
Moderate

Highway 99 becomes Main Street as you enter the town of Ashland from the northeast or southwest. Cowslip's Belle is on the right side of Main Street two blocks north of the Shakespeare Festival.

I found Cowslip's Belle after an infuriating day of 110-degree heat, an overheated car that refused to stay cool unless I ran the heater full blast, and a sunburnt driver's-side arm and thigh that I had to cover with a jacket to keep from blistering. To say the least, in this mood, nothing could possibly have struck me as romantic. In fact, I was certain that any place I stayed would add fuel to the fire. Only a place like Cowslip's Belle could (and did) facilitate a change of attitude from delirium to delight.

Located two blocks from the town and theatre district, this bed & breakfast is where other bed & breakfast owners come to find out how to do it right. Here, the attention to your needs is reassuring when things are going wrong and helpful when things are going right. The rooms provide you the best night's sleep possible in a firm but somehow cushy four-poster sigh of relief, under the softest quilts to ever touch your skin. The bathrooms are beautifully done in shiny green and black tiles and the bedroom furnishings are unique and enviable. Breakfast is a fiesta of fruit, French toast, yogurt and home-baked scones.

♦ **ROMANTIC EATING:** Ask anyone in Ashland where the best food is served and they are likely to mention the **Winchester Inn, 35 South Second Street, Ashland 97520, (503) 488-1113** (Brunch/Moderate; Dinner/Expensive). Maybe they will also tell you the restaurant is on the main floor of a renovated Queen Anne-style home, with tables placed casually throughout the library, living room and dining alcove and plenty of privacy-space in between. The windows look out onto gardens surrounding the building, and the mood is always cordial and relaxed.

Music To Suit The Heart

I was at a wedding recently and the music the wedding party and bride walked down the aisle to was an opera singer's rendition of Billy Joel's *"Don't Go Changin'"* and Bette Midler's *"The Rose."* As I watched the women in gossamer pink float by in ceremonious procession, I thought to myself, "This is the strangest, most unromantic music to have at a wedding." The refrain in Billy Joel's song is, *"How long will it take until you believe in me, the way that I believe in you?"* Sounds like a one-way relationship to me. Hardly what I would call a reciprocation of feelings.

Bette Midler's *"The Rose"* is even more fatalistic. It is an existential song about a drug addict's potential promise of recovery — if not during the spring when the roses bloom, then next year, after the death of winter when the roses bloom once again. Except in the movie she doesn't recover, she dies. Now isn't that romantic? More like heartburn than heartthrob if you ask me. But then that's the whole point. They didn't ask me, they went with their feeling about what was lyrical and meaningful to their ears, and not to anyone else's.

So whether it be the Beatles, Beethoven, Van Halen, Sondheim, Billy Ocean, the Philadelphia Philharmonic or the melodious tones of your own voices singing off-key, what's important is that you choose what you like, for any romantic occasion — a wedding, drive in the car or jogging together with headphones — and everyone else can keep their opinions to themselves. And note — that includes finding out what each of you likes and making a compromise. Nothing could be more off the mark than to play Frank Zappa when it's Frank Sinatra one of you is yearning for.

continues

The above listings are arranged alphabetically. The following descriptions are arranged around the City Center and then south.

> *"Life is just one fool thing after another; love is just two fool things after each other."*
>
> Anon

PORTLAND

Once you visit this city, it is likely you too will become a Portland enthusiast. The Portland area provides a truly fabulous selection of everything you could want in a blend of a city-and-country-type courtship. It abounds in an amazing variety of terrain for walking, hiking or dawdling, and possesses a rose garden that is one of the most majestic in the world, nonpareil restaurants, countless acres of forest and enough greenery to give new meaning to the word nature-lover. This is a city with patience and a dedication to making life a little better here than anywhere else.

The local flavor and charm of Portland's Nob Hill (a diversified and quaint shopping neighborhood), the growing downtown and the renovated lane of distinctive restaurants and hotels called Riverplace, balance beautifully with the city's multitude of parks and forests. Whether you are visiting for a day or a short or long time, this city's appeal will be felt and is bound to create a loving lasting impression.

THE HERON HAUS

2545 N.W. Westover Road, Portland 97201
(503) 274-1846
Moderate to Very Expensive

Please call for reservations and directions.

Bed & breakfasts all have their own special personalities for conveying the cordial, cozy warmth that is essential to this genre of lodging. And given the right touches, there is nothing quite as affection-producing as staying in a home that has diligently tended to matters of the heart and senses. That includes the aroma of just-baked morning pastries, a roaring fireplace, cushy furnishings, snuggly quilts covering over-sized pillows and a conspicuous amount of tender loving care. The Heron Haus has all this and more.

This is a huge (7,500 square feet), stately mansion used almost entirely for guests. Add to this setting and the array of comforts, a sun deck, pool and ample suites, and you have the makings of a memorable stay. There is one other feature I forgot to mention: the bathrooms. In fact, you may decide to stay in there and forget about ever returning to your room. One suite has a Jacuzzi that overlooks the city, and another has a shower with seven nozzles, covering every inch of you with pulsating water. With space to spare, Heron Haus can accommodate couples who want to emerge clean, giggling and inseparable.

PAISLEY'S

1204 N.W. 21st, Portland 97209
(503) 243-2403
Dessert Only — Very Reasonable

From downtown Portland take N.W. Lovejoy Street west to 21st Avenue and turn left. Paisley's is at the intersection of Northrup Street and 21st.

Paisley's is dedicated to the dessert lovers of the world, emphasizing love and chocolate. The menu changes daily, with a parade of offerings that are as delicious to hear described as to eat. The aroma of robust cappuccinos and the delicate souffles, tortes, tarts, brulees and on and on will sweep you off your feet. So will the attention the owners have given to creating a simple, attractive place where you can spoil yourselves silly. The demure restaurant is filled with handsome wood tables in an honest Northwest setting. Paisley's is a worthwhile sweet place to stop and exchange sweet nothings.

♦ **ROMANTIC OPTIONS:** Paisley's is located in the heart of Portland's **Nob Hill,** which is blessed with over 40 lovingly renovated neighborhood shops and no less than four dozen restaurants, each one more interesting than the last. From end to end this enticing procession has everything two curious consumers shopping to fulfill the heart could want.

CAFE DES AMIS

1987 N.W. Kearney Street, Portland 97209
(503) 295-6487
Moderate to Expensive

Take N.W. Lovejoy west to 19th Avenue and turn south for one block to Kearney Street. The cafe is at the intersection of Kearney and 19th.

It isn't easy to blend a Northwest atmosphere with French cuisine and come up with an effective coexistence. Yet at Cafe des Amis, the two concepts work beautifully together and the food is a gastronomic treat. The simplicity of the room, with wood tables well-spaced from each other, and the cordial, easy feeling all about make possible a total romantic-culinary experience. Just the right effects make this one of Portland's masterstrokes of dining.

SKYLINE DRIVE

Portland's Forest Park is a vast wilderness on the west side of the Willamette River. At the park's south end, Cornell Road intersects with Skyline Drive. Skyline Drive borders the east side of the park.

Is it possible for city roads or highways to spiral up and around to celestial planes of visual splendor? If so, Skyline Drive is a candidate, and a quick or slow drive over this winding road will help you cast a deciding vote.

The road is embroidered with miles of fascinating vistas that can revitalize the urban-weary traveler. It outlines the eastern boundary of Forest Park, independently following a course up the hillside. At the crest you can view the incredible contour of the Cascades, the valley awash in colors of green, the gentle forms of the Coastal Mountain Range and the city of Portland. If you want the option of getting up and away without having to go far from the city, cruise Skyline Drive any time of day or night.

♦ *ROMANTIC SUGGESTION:* Along Skyline Drive there is a grade school, **Skyline School,** located at 11536 N.W. It is also smack-dab atop this marvelous scenic road, and when school isn't in session, it is a fairly isolated setting. The playground in front of the school slopes down to the road. Here, a swing or a slide is classic equipment for courtship. A short return to younger attitudes and the cinematic sunset are worth a brief romp through recess.

MacMaster House
Bed & Breakfast

1041 S.W. Vista Avenue, Portland 97205
(503) 223-7362
Very Reasonable to Moderate

Call for reservations and directions.

While in Portland negotiate your plans to include a stay at MacMaster House. This turn-of-the-century mansion fancifully accents the nearby city center and glorious Washington Park. Through this impressive bed & breakfast you'll see and feel the genteel style of grand, old-world living.

As you walk up to the house, the formal portico with Doric columns and Palladian windows of leaded glass at first seems Colonial and stiff, yet, once inside, there is a bright, airy feeling all around. The suites are handsome and lush, with fireplaces and separate sitting areas, and the MacMaster Suite has a deck with a view. The rooms will invite you to spend the evening together reviewing your relaxed time in Portland.

WASHINGTON PARK
ROSE GARDENS

From downtown Portland, drive west on W. Burnside, following the signs to the Rose Gardens.

Washington Park will strike you as the perfect *lovers'-lane* hideout. The road to the tree-shaded parking area winds up a long, steep hill to a summit, where the park serves as a bastion of peace over the city and Willamette Valley. From the fragrant, endless rows of rose bushes to the exotic Japanese Gardens and the unhindered view of Portland and the mountains beyond, this is pure embracing territory, acre after magnificent acre.

The park is styled like a Shakespearean amphitheatre. Trimmed hedges and multicolored blooming roses serve as the proscenium arch around the sloping hill, opening to a backdrop of uninterrupted afternoons, brilliant sunsets or twinkling evening lights. The grounds are adorned with gardens that perenially endure the seasons. Romeo and Juliet never had it as good as you will here at Washington Park.

MACLEAY PARK

Macleay Park is one of many entrances to Portland's Forest Park. You can enter Macleay off the Thurman Bridge near Franklin and 32nd Street N.W., or at the end of Forest Park in Northwest Portland off Cornell Road.

Macleay Park is a park within a park. It is just one of the almost limitless doorways into Portland's immense back yard called Forest Park. The latter is regarded as the largest city-wilderness in the United States, and it affords enough kissing places that if you're not careful, you can risk a lip or two.

Macleay Park is a gorgeous example of the enclaves of nature that thrive amid the city, giving testimony to the ability of urban and country life to coexist in harmony. You enter at one end, leaving the city world behind totally, and exit at the other end to find the city there again to welcome you back. In between you will have passed through a wooded utopia — a lush green wilderness strewn with surging creeks and hiking trails.

NOTE: Collin's Sanctuary is another doorway into Forest Park, and not very well-known even though its intrinsic, secluded beauty is near the heart of the city. This is a bird sanctuary and part of Portland's Audubon Society. Call them for information about Collin's Sanctuary.

HEATHMAN HOTEL'S TEA COURT

Broadway at Salmon Street, Portland 97205
(503) 241-4100
Moderate

Look for clearly marked signs on Highway 405 for Market Street or City Center. Market and Broadway intersect; turn north onto Broadway. Salmon Street is a few blocks north.

When you walk into the lobby of the Heathman Hotel, your first impression will be one of Northwest skepticism. This hesitation will be due primarily to the geometric art and stark, marble detailing. While the appearance may be distinguished and striking, the modern design and hard finishes create a cold feeling and don't lend themselves to coziness. In direct contrast, next to the lobby, a dignified wood stairway draws you into an entirely different room, where the Tea Court waits patiently.

The classic decor, solid wood paneling and the genial quiet here make this a suitable place for an afternoon of thoughtful conversation and warm gazes together. The bright fire and the small art collection lining the balcony wall will enhance your exchange.

ROMANTIC WARNING: With regard to the Heathman Hotel as a place to stay: It is quite well-known, but keep in mind that it is just a hotel — nice, but not romantic.

ATWATER'S RESTAURANT

111 S.W. Fifth Avenue, Portland 97204
(503) 220-3629
Very Expensive

On Fifth and Burnside in downtown Portland at the top of the U.S.
Bancorp Tower. From Highway 405, follow the City Center exit to Fourth
Avenue. Turn north on Fourth Avenue and west on Pine Street. This
will take you to a parking garage under the building.

Atwater's Restaurant, atop Portland's tallest building, proclaims
that it is designed like an exclusive uptown residence. Upon entering
you will understand why. High-brow pageantry and detail prevail
throughout. From the Oriental-style elevator doors to the silver
service, marble buffets and floor and other extravagant finishing
touches, it is clear that this is an ultra-formal dining establishment.
When you finally look beyond the embellishments, your eyes will
focus on the floor-to-ceiling windows that disclose what sitting on
cloud nine really is like.

At twilight, while you sip a glass of wine, the urban world beneath
you is slowly shadowed as the sunlight fades and disappears behind
the distant mountains. All this heavenly grandeur serves as a potent
backdrop to the interior. If fancy dining with a ringside view of the
world is something you can get into, this is the place to try it on for
size — and of course, one size fits two very nicely.

NOTE: Sunday brunch is a lavish eating experience at Atwater's.

RIVERPLACE

1510 S.W. Harbor Way, Portland 97201
Expensive to Very Expensive

From downtown Portland take S.W. Market Street east to the river, where it will dead-end at Riverplace.

Personally I do not find Riverplace the least bit romantic. I can't imagine, from a Northwest frame of reference, how a 1/2-mile-long arcade of nouveau-lifestyle renovated stores and restaurants could be intimate and endearing. Still, in all fairness, when I went to visit this Willamette River development, I saw enough couples strolling hand in hand that I decided to include Riverplace and objectively give a perspective on romance that is not wholeheartedly my own.

Riverplace begins with the European refinement and poshness of the **Alexis Hotel** at the northern tip of the walk. Here you have an exquisite European-styled building with quality accommodations and a distinctive, well-received restaurant. Farther down, as you walk along with the water on one side and a series of handsome condominiums on the other, there are a dozen or so boutiques, eateries and cafes. Still farther are more restaurants with water views and there is even a restaurant set out in the middle of the water. Admittedly this is a lovely development and there are enough options here that there is surely something for everyone regardless of taste or budget. In any case, Riverplace is worth a stroll and perhaps a stop somewhere along the way for a glass of wine or a shot of espresso, a quick disco beat, and whatever else may be alive and happening along this uptown Portland landmark.

SAUVIE ISLAND

Go north on Highway 30 to the Sauvie Island Bridge, about 11 miles from downtown Portland.

When you feel the need for the wide-open, empty spaces, driving to this vast pastoral oasis is the perfect choice. Sauvie Island is a popular Portland getaway, but its size prevents it from ever feeling crowded. There are miles of isolated beaches and numerous hikes through wetlands, pasture, oak woodlands and spotty sections of coniferous forest. Oak Island is a much smaller landmass, attached by a natural bridge at the northeast end of Sauvie Island, where stretches of sandy beach are available.

ROMANTIC WARNING: Sauvie Island can be covered in smog when other parts of the area are clear. Check the horizon before setting out for the island. Also there is no drinking water or gasoline available there.

TRYON CREEK STATE PARK

Head south from Portland on Interstate 5 to the Terwilliger exit. Travel 2 1/2 miles due south on S.W. Terwilliger Boulevard to get to the park.

Come to Tryon Creek State Park when you want to immerse yourself in forest that isn't wilderness, or too arduous to handle. This is the place for easy walks along gently rolling, red-bark paths through thick forestland. Don't expect wide vistas or places to sit in the sun. It is almost always shady and moist here, not to mention a little muddy in the winter. But whether you walk for miles or for just a few hundred feet, the two of you will feel safe, unhurried and alone here, speaking words of devotion and love to be heard by no one else.

YAMHILL WINE COUNTRY

A 45-minute drive southwest from Portland will bring you smack-dab into wine country: pastoral rolling hills, pastures of golden grass and rows of grapes twined around poles to help their growth toward the sun. There are a number of wineries interspersed throughout this picturesque landscape, each one with its own charisma and attitude about what makes a good glass of wine. Whether or not you are wine connoisseurs, there is a calm and harmony throughout the Yamhill countryside that can be meaningful for both of you.

If you are a veteran wine-taster, then you have Shangri-la at hand. As you gallivant from winery to winery sampling the various proud offerings of each vineyard, you will have the opportunity to engage in a virtually all-day non-stop picnic. The only things you need to remember are the mandatory supplies of cheese, French bread, smoked salmon, raw veggies and fresh fruit, particularly apples, strawberries, melons and peaches.

The dozen or so wineries of the Yamhill Valley each boast a robust wine selection, a rathskeller tasting room and a reposeful country setting that adds to your palate's experience. Some of these cellars are antique-laden homes, others are crowned by tantalizing views and idyllic gardens, while still others are plain buildings with row after row of grapevines. Whether you choose to visit one or all, and whether you choose to imbibe or not, your entire winery-hopping jaunt will be an *intoxicating* joy.

◆ *ROMANTIC SUGGESTIONS:* **Tualatin Vineyards on Seavey Road, Route 1, Box 339, Forest Grove 97116, (503) 357-5005,** and **Elk Cove Vineyards on 27751 N.W. Olson Road, Gaston 97119, (503) 985-7760,** are two Elysian and exceptional wineries in Yamhill County. They will perfectly accentuate this dream-like country outing.

◆ **ROMANTIC OPTIONS:** As you tryst about the tasting rooms, you may want to stretch out your visit for an extra day. To keep with the spirit of the area, a pleasant, congenial bed & breakfast is an understandable benefit. The best way to tend to that need is to stay either at the **Owl's View Bed & Breakfast, P.O. Box 732, Newberg 97132, (503) 538-6498** (Reasonable to Expensive), or the **Orchard View Inn, 16540 N.W. Orchard View Road, McMinnville 97128, (503) 472-0165** (Reasonable to Very Moderate). The Owl's View sits on a hill overlooking the valley and the Orchard View is nestled in a country neighborhood with deer prancing around the back yard.

SCENE-HOPPING RECOMMENDATIONS: Spend a day touring Portland's city life, shopping on **Nob Hill** and downtown. Then splurge and have lunch or an appetizer at **Atwater's.** Just before sunset venture out to **Washington Park** and enjoy the splendor of the **Rose Gardens.** Retire to your room at **The Heron Haus** and take a long soak in your own hot tub. In the late morning, after breakfast, drive out to the **Yamhill wineries** and spend the day relishing the fruit of the vine. At day's end either stay at one of the Yamhill B&Bs or return to Portland for an uptown outing at **Riverplace.**

AUXILIARY READING

62 Hiking Trails of the Northern Oregon Cascades, by Don and Roberta Lowe

100 Hikes in the North Cascades, by Ira Spring and Harvey Manning

Touring the Wine Country of Oregon, by Ronald and Glenda Holden

102 Hikes in the Alpine Lakes, Southern Cascades and Olympics, by Ira Spring and Harvey Manning

103 Hikes in Southwestern British Columbia, published by The Mountaineers Books

50 Hikes in the Mount Rainier National Park, by Ira Spring and Harvey Manning

Write to **The Mountaineers Books at 306 Second Avenue W., Seattle, WA 98119, 1-(800) 553-4453,** for their full catalogue of Northwest outdoor books.

Oregon Free, by Kiki Canniff

Washington Free, by Kiki Canniff

> *"It just takes an attitude change to turn the delirium into delight."*
>
> Me